Engineering

My Future

David E.S. Middleton

Published by D.E.S. Middleton 2020

Publisher contact e mail: dmech40@yahoo.co.uk
RRP paperback £9.00   p&p uk £2.00 (2020)
ISBN: 978-0-9933826-2-8

Printed by Book Printing UK
Remus House, Coltsfoot Drive, Peterborough

Contents

Illustrations

To Florence

Shall I compare thee to a summer's day?
Thou art more lovely and more temperate:
Rough winds do shake the darling buds of May,
And summer's lease hath too short a date:*

- Ex Sonnet No 18 William Shakespeare

Foreword

The purpose of this book is to leave some marker of the path that one Engineer took through the jungle of professional life. I enjoyed the privileges, open to others, of an engineering training at a time when it was normal to accept small payment while learning on the job. There were opportunities to learn more at Dundee Technical College and an informed Government awarded grants for fee free higher Education for those showing promise. The degrees earned were not an assurance of success but were "tickets to dance"; one still had to learn the steps.

The story below is self-explanatory; suffice it to say that the list of people who helped me in my life would be long indeed and I owe them a large debt of gratitude.

Acknowledgements

I wish to thank my son Edward and niece Kim for their assistance in editing this work.

I also wish to thank my family for putting up with me during the pursuit of my engineering career.

Thanks to staff of Dundee City Archives and Dundee University Archives for their help and support.

Part 1 1940-1956

Early Days

I was born in the house at 25 Blacklock Crescent Dundee in the then new housing estate of Linlathen. This estate comprised Canadian cedar clad houses and building of the scheme had started in 1939 finishing in 1940 or thereby presumably due to wartime conditions i.e. shortage of materials and labour. The estate is situated in the North East district of Dundee Scotland alongside Pitkerro Road. My full name is David Edward Shepherd Middleton; David from my uncle David Shepherd and Edward from great grandfather Edward Galloway. My mother's name was Jane Shepherd Middleton and my father was Robert Samuel Middleton.

I am told that I was born at home and in something of a hurry. The event was recorded by my father on to the underside of the stairway of the four roomed semi-detached house. The family took shelter there during air raids which explains the odd location of the pencilled note. These houses were state of the council house art at the time with a living room, bathroom, kitchen and three bedrooms upstairs. The kitchen had a larder, a coal bunker and a gas fired clothes boiler. The living room had storage cupboards and the space under the stairs known by some as the lumber room. The living room was furnished with a couch and two easy chairs in varying states of repair, a sideboard of 1920's vintage, a dining table and hand chairs and the piano which sat on four green jelly

1

like glass insulators. There was electricity for lighting, one power point for the wireless and one in each of the bedrooms for limited heating i.e. a small portable electric fire. There was gas in the kitchen for the cooker and clothes boiler. The living room floor had a linoleum covering and two rugs. Elsewhere in the house linoleum covered the floors. Outside there was garden front, side and back. This was a massive upgrade from a two room tenement flat at 37 Rosefield Street Dundee with no inside toilet or bathroom, for a then family of parents and five children comprising three daughters and two sons. The family was spread over the years 1923 to my birth on 24th August 1940 so I became number six and Nancy was to follow in 1944. At the time of my birth the Battle of Britain was being fought over the South East of England and bombing of major cities was happening. The London blitz had started on 23rd August 1940 and the bombing would spread to major centres of population.

Dundee did have some minor raids and sadly there were casualties but overall it was to be one of the safer places to live for the duration. However I am told that one bomb landed on Linlathen that 1940 summer and in the Middleton household my father and mother were at home as was my elder brother Robert and visiting grandma Middleton. The whistle of the bomb was clearly heard and my father dived to the floor no doubt a reflex conditioned by experience in world war one. Robert followed him and my grandmother reportedly sat motionless through the emergency. The bomb narrowly missed houses at the West end of Glenconner drive and exploded in a field nearby.

Clearly my memories of that early time are non-existent but it seems that plenty was going on round me lying there in blissful ignorance. My father was a locomotive fitter on the LMS

2

railway at the Dundee West engine shed. He would be 43 at the start of the war and in a reserved occupation working steady shift work and also served on the railway fire service and ARP at work. He told me that at the start of the war in September 1939 when invasion was a probability an order was received at the engine shed to hide the locomotive special repair tools by burying at sites round the shed. These would include jacks, spanners, lifting aids, levers etc. However nobody thought to map out the location of the hidden tools and thereafter difficulties arose when the special tools were required. Some items are probably still buried there. His transport to work was by bicycle and otherwise by tram from Maryfield to Roseangle. Buses to Linlathen were available later. He took a piece (sandwich) for lunch and always brought back the wrapping paper and string every day. These were economy measures which as far as I know continued to his retirement in 1963. A sound I remember in the evening was the distant roar of a steam locomotive, possibly a 2-8-0 WD class, hauling a heavy southbound train up the bank on to the Tay Bridge and it would give a hoot on its whistle. If my father was on the backshift we would say "that's Dad!" - though he was not a driver. The hoot was probably the driver signalling to the banking engine to stop pushing.

My mother had her hands full in keeping house for us and this would include the weekly wash day on Wednesday when the gas wash boiler would be lit and the boiling clothes stirred with a stout pole this being part of a shunter's pole from the railway. There was a wash sink and a deep sink in the kitchen. My mother volunteered to act as a first aider. This was a wartime measure as part of Air Raid Precautions (ARP). As far as I know there were never any bomb casualties to see to but there were several minor cuts and bruises for children of the locality, including those of our

3

own family. I probably owe my life to the fact that this first aid was available to stem the loss of blood from a severed artery I sustained from falling on to barbed wire. My sister Rena also suffered a bad gash to her leg from stumbling over a large stone in the blackout.

I was unaware of the blackout, or rather it was the everyday practice, but it was in force with the gas street lights never on and blackout curtains or panels in place over all windows after dark.

Living in the house in 1940 in addition to my parents were Ella 18, Edie 15, Robbie 13, Rena 10, Donnie 4 and the black cat. Ella and Edie were working, Ella in a textile factory and Edie at clerical work although they would both change their jobs as the war progressed. Ella would join the ATS and Edie had to move her clerical work to an essential industry namely Moncur's factory Victoria Jute Works in Ure Street Dundee. The others were at school or at home pre-school.

As I grew I became more aware of my environment and earliest memories probably date from 1943 but of course dating at that age is unreliable. My world was at floor level and I was aware of the daily fire cleaning out and fire-lighting routine, the dust motes floating around in the sunlight, the underside of the table and severe restrictions on my freedom to roam beyond the outside doorway.

After learning to walk I did escape from time to time and I remember seeing tracked army vehicles passing down Pitkerro Road, evidence of the Polish army units which were billeted in various country houses outside Dundee.

Being the bairn in the house I no doubt received the care and attention of my sisters and their friends. I particularly remember Ella being in army uniform and her bringing a nice friend "Ginger" while on leave. I learned later in life that that particular leave was of the French variety and MPs turned up at the house to remove the AWOL offenders.

They were taken to the house known as the "Hollies" in Broughty Ferry and after a night in captivity they were marched in the gutter along Ferry Road to Dundee railway station and returned to their camp near Preston. Ella gave the reason for leaving the camp to be the dreadful conditions she had to endure including rising at 4am to set the coal fires for cooking on field kitchens for a great many troops then amassing round the country in preparation for D day. This involved getting up very early to get the snow covered coal in to the cookhouse and trying to get a good fire going. She made her point and there was some improvement in the arrangements.

Another story of Ella involved race relations at the camp at Preston. The US army provided a cookhouse orderly to help out and on one occasion this was a black private. A white US army officer come into the cookhouse and scored a line on the floor and said the private was not to cross it. Ella, being the sergeant cook in charge soon told the US officer to get out of her kitchen and that she made the rules there! She also told me that she and her ATS friend used to go to Blackpool for an evening's entertainment. On one occasion when returning to catch the Preston train they got talking to the engine driver and the girls were allowed to travel on the footplate to Preston.

Ella had married early in the war to a Royal Navy sailor Vincent Hand. The war however had separated them and like many wartime marriages it ended with divorce.

During the time their marriage lasted Vincent would appear at our house on leave. He would bring to my mother presents of things that the Navy had and civvies did not. This included a large carton of boxes of matches which I was allowed to play with in front of the fire. Not a good idea but luckily no accident happened and my mother probably spirited them away before anyone was hurt.

As I grew out of infancy I became aware of things like money and sweets both of which were in short supply. My brother Donnie would tantalise me with stories of how cheap sweets were "before the war" that phrase being much used by everyone.

Particularly noticeable and disappointing were the inoperative and quite empty chocolate bar machines in stations and outside shops.

As I approached school age of five years the war came to a conclusion and there was much partying. Near to our house was a square and a large bonfire was arranged to celebrate the peace. Sticking out of the top of the fire were two long poles with flags.

One flag was a German Nazi swastika and the other had an image of Winston Churchill. Such was the mixture of feelings at the time.

A major event in 1945 in my experience was my sister Edie's wedding. She had met Canadian soldier Gerald Strome who had visited our Shepherd grandparents' home on being posted to the UK earlier in the war. Gerald's home town was Winnipeg Manitoba where my uncle Harry Shepherd lived; thus the connection.

The wedding was held in St Mary's church Nethergate and thereafter in the restaurant of the Green's Playhouse cinema. Green's Playhouse cinema was a wonderful art deco place; colourful, luxurious warm and with an appetising aroma emanating from the restaurant tearoom next to the large foyer. At five years old and in a world of shortages and rationing the wedding meal was very much appreciated especially the piece of cake with, a new taste, marzipan. I have liked marzipan ever since.

Our Family

While I was about to go to school and the second world war had just ended our family situation was as follows. My father was a fitter on the LMS railway Dundee West Locomotive shed off Magdalen Yard Road. My mother was a housewife at home and had been so since the birth of Ella in 1923. Ella was living with us with her son Michael and she worked at various jobs in local industry. Edie was working in a textile factory, Moncur's, as a clerkess, Robbie was a clerk in a solicitors office about to go into the Navy on National Service, Rena was working with the Ministry of Food meat distribution office, Donnie was at St Michaels School, I was about to go to Linlathen infants School and Nancy was approaching one year old as the bairn of the family. The progress of the family is material for another work and the above will suffice for now.

The Neighbours

Neighbours change as time goes by so the following is somewhat time based.

The other half of our semi was occupied by the Baillies. Mrs Baillie was a middle aged single parent. I do not know much about Mr Baillie other than he was probably of French nationality and was not present. The family comprised daughter Lucy and sons Charlie and George. These were a grown up family; in the mid 1940's the youngest George would be about 20, Charlie would be in his mid twenties and Lucy older than the sons. Charlie was a heaterboy, i.e. a heater of rivets, at Caledon Shipyard where George also worked as a general labourer.

In that direction, i.e. increasing house numbers, were the Connor family then the Appleyards.

In the other direction were The Murrays comprising Mr (Peter), a man of many skills, Mrs (Maggie) Murray a woman with business ability and a generous person, Mary, Isa, Margaret, Helen, Rose and Anne and the lads Tommy, Pat and Bennie. Next door to them were the Quins, then Cooper, Low and Tennant these latter being in the "Squarie" which was a useful play area. My play pals would be from the families Murray, Snowden, Dunn, Brown, Hodge, Cochrane, Quinn , McLennan.

In most of these families the mother was at home and the father worked but in some cases both parents worked and the kids had to use the 'key on a string' for entry.

Violence in the area was rare but drunkenness was common and usually at weekends. At New Year time internal family squabbles could result in injuries. There were family alliances for example the Coopers , Glasses and Kerrs were said to be related. Some fathers were unemployed but this was usually due to disability from injury at war or workplace. Various trades were represented, Mr Connor carter, Mr Quinn Palace Theatre stage manager, Mr Tennant joiner, Mr McLennan quarry worker, Mr Brown bookie, Mr McGuinness craneman, Mr Snowden riveter, Mr Cochrane Co-op grocer. Others were manual workers of various kinds but there were few clerical and retail workers other than daughters.

Friendships varied from time to time and I had no long term friendship with one person.

This was normal as activities varied with the season and the current interests e.g. football, cricket, fishing, the berry harvest, the potato harvest or illness, family requirements, holidays and school.

Things changed as families moved away, friends grew out of one's age bracket, new people moved in.

I found little of what I was interested in was shared with my contemporaries. I was a stamp collector, I gathered small stones from the excavations taking place for the school being built nearby. I was interested in railway locomotives and trains, aeroplanes and vehicles.

I would go off by myself to the library at Arthurstone terrace and borrow books. But this was a life apart from my play friends. Interactions with friends were rarely about knowledge based things or based on any hobby or enthusiasm. There were a couple of joint interests eg in stamp collecting and crystal making but these were short lived in my friend's cases.

Activity with pals was more hands-on playing cowboys and indians, cops and robbers or street games such as kick the can, hide and seek and question and answer games such as Film stars. The main interests among my friends were telling jokes, kicking things, throwing things, breaking things, setting small fires, playing football and generally fighting. In good weather there might be a trip to the countryside e.g. "the gourdies" This was a broom covered area on the Ballumbie farm to the North east of our home patch. This had grassy clearings and rocky bits which were ideal for cowboy and Indian games.

Then there were the "pictures" ie the cinema. Dundee had 22 cinemas active in the 1940's. There were the downtown cinemas such as Greens Playhouse, Kinnaird, La Scala, Gaumont and the Vic. In our east end the district cinemas were The Royal and the Broadway both in Arthurstone Terrace, The Royalty in Watson St, The Cinema in Morgan St, The Tivoli in Bonnybank Rd, The Odeon at Coldside and The New Palladium in Alexander St. One of these would be visited about once per week.

The Murray boys had a sister Isa who worked in the Greens Playhouse in Nethergate (now rebuilt after a fire as Mecca bingo) which was a magnificent art deco building with a cafe and had the second largest capacity in Europe said to be in excess of 4000. The entrance was via multiple doors to a ticket office then on to a Terrazo floor with art deco ornamentation. This generous hall led to a central wide staircase with side features in rainbow coloured back lit reeded glass. The staircase was used for access to the circle and boxes. Particularly impressive were the blue green pink and yellow coloured ceramic toilet facilities. Isa received free passes as a concession and on a few occasions I was asked along to a free visit to this opulent cinema. Favourite films were based on cowboys, aeroplanes, fencing, cops and robbers, Al Jolson, the Bowery Boys, Ma and Pa Kettles and cartoons. Drama and romantic pictures were shunned .

Sundays were especially dull. People did not appear much before lunchtime. One frosty February Sunday in the late 1940's there was not much to do after lunchtime and the Murray boys, Pat and Benny, were sent to take the "best butter" to their auntie Kate who lived in John Street downtown Dundee. I was asked if I wanted to go and I agreed as long as they paid the fare which would be about 2 pence each way. We set off to catch a No 16 bus which took us to Victoria Road. We then walked along Dudhope Street which became Barrack Road then the Barrack Park otherwise known as Dudhope Park. There was a cold frosty haze about which was thickened by the smoke from the many domestic chimneys in the town. The driveway up to the castle from Barrack Street was on a level with the chimney pots of the houses in John Street below and the smoke from these chimneys added to and clung to the still frosty air of that Sunday afternoon. At Dudhope castle there was an aviary with exotic birds which were fed with stale bread by the park strollers and local urchins.

We watched two Territorial soldiers who were cleaning out a shed on the barrack square outside the old officer's quarters of Dudhope castle. National servicemen had to spend two years in the Territorial army after demob. Among the stuff being binned were what looked like hand grenades, perhaps practice ones. The officers' quarters were in a large Georgian building which was probably once grand but was now the shabby home to squatter families. This is a reminder of the severe shortage of housing post war.

We then descended to John Street to find Kate's house in the warren of run down tenements.

This was typical of Dundee's poor tenement housing. The common stair led to wooden floored landing and then out to a back plettie (or platform) with doors thereon to the flatted dwellings. There was in the area a smell of decay and a poorly lit atmosphere of depression, it seemed to me. However Auntie Kate's house was pleasant warm and welcoming and the boys exchanged a half pound of best butter (ie actual butter) for a pound of butter (ie margarine). This exchange made sense as the Murray's were a large family and Kate lived on her own in her

11

room and kitchen. We probably got a cup of tea and a plain biscuit before finding our way out to the Lochee Road and on to Pole Street where another relative lived. This was a two storey building but still old and basic but we were warmly received and sat and talked with two visiting young girls "on holiday from Glasgow" one of whom was called Pearl. The Murrays had hailed from Glasgow in a former generation during the period when Dundee had a demand for mill workers. Their original home in Dundee had been in the Polepark-Brook Street area and these girls were from the Murrays' Glasgow relatives.

After refreshment we made our way down Polepark Road and had a look at the "ten storey land" in the Burn area which was an awesome sight to us. Our journey then included Balfour Street then on through a close into Airlie Place and the Perth Road. We caught a tram in Perth road to Maryfield and walked from there back to Linlathen. Thus was spent a useful Sunday afternoon and it was just as well it was cold for the sake of the margarine and the butter.

The Neighbourhood

There were two large housing schemes built in the 1930's at the north east end of the city of Dundee namely Mid Craigie and Linlathen. Mid Craigie was the earlier being built in two developments; the slated tenement houses and the red roofed terraced houses. It was said that the reason for Mid Craigie was "slum clearance" and that of Linlathen was "overcrowding" the latter being considered socially more desirable (by the latter's residents of course). Whether this was true or not did not alter the fact that most people in both estates were good hard working families with a need for the decent housing which these schemes did provide.

The schemes were built on ground sloping down in a north easterly direction to the Dighty burn valley. Mid Craigie lay to the south of Pitkerro Road and Linlathen to the North. Pitkerro Road was an ancient road leading out of Dundee to the agricultural hinterland and farms and estates such as Pitkerro, Linlathen (not the housing estate), Greenfield, Whitfield, Ballumbie, Drumgieth, Baldovie and Barns of Wedderburn.

Industry already in the area included Cargill's Midmill Bleachfield, Angus County's Longhaugh quarry and Foreman's bag reclamation works at the "Snuff mill" near Happyhillock (more correctly Craigie mill).

Midmill had two industrial residential units belonging to the Midmill bleachfield or bleachworks namely Midmill Parkhead which was a three storey tenement and Midmill Terrace which was a two storey tenement range with garrets. These had been built probably in Victorian times. The terrace had toilets in outhouses while Parkhead enjoyed indoor toilets. There was a small weatherboard shop at Parkhead run by the Lowrie family and this was the main local retail facility the next being the shops at Pitkerro Road/Kingsway circle where there was Mastersons draper, A.G Kidd baker, Wilson's newspaper shop, Johnstons stores, a chemist a greengrocer, Findlays small grocers, a post office and Joe Zacharini's chip shop.

The Midmill bleachfield had ponds associated with it which were fed by a lade (the wee burnie) off the Dichty burn near the Forfar Road Mains toll. There was a sluice gate off the Dichty just to the east of the Forfar Road bridge at Mains toll and this led to the wee burnie. The first mill it served was New Mains mill which was a ruin in the 1940's but the water wheel could still be seen from the path looking down on the mill.

Downstream this burn fed Honeygreen ponds below the aqueduct crossing the Dichty valley after which it fed a large pond for Cargill's Midmill bleachfield. Below this pond there were ruins of an earlier bleachfield works, Fountainbleau?, to the West of Midmill bleachfield works.

The proper name for Midmill Bleachworks was Dundee Bleachworks.

The wee burnie then continued for a bit before disappearing into Midmill Bleachworks reappearing to the east to feed the ruinous Craigie mill otherwise known as the Snuff mill. This mill showed signs of being burned out but there was a community connected with it. Textile operations were carried out here by a Mr Forman in low buildings and there were cotter houses and a few more superior houses. The work carried out here was jute bag manufacture and recycling comprising repairs and washing of sacks.

This might not seem worthwhile but Mr Forman did drive around in a Rolls Royce car.

The wee burnie then rejoined its parent Dichty burn just before the entrance to Parkhead football ground. Beyond the football ground was the Dighty burn with a weir and a bridge. The weir had fed the Douglasfield bleachworks now in ruin since closing around 1900.

These areas were to form part of the play environment.

There was a card gambling activity which took place usually on Sundays. This was a movable event and was illegal; an eye kept open for the police. This was an adult activity and was based on the card game Banker but known locally as Punts.

As one comes down Pitkerro Road at the lower end there was the Parkhead Midmill tenement on the right and the land from there to the dighty burn bounded by Happyhillock Road and Pitkerro Road was Bleachworks owned. After Parkhead there was the WRI hall then some old warehouses, then Midmill terrace before the Bleachworks proper. The card school would be in the area of these warehouses or in a horse's shed to the rear of Midmill terrace. The horse, if in residence, would be gently pushed out of the shed and a roll of old linoleum laid on the floor. On Fountainbleau Drive to the west of Midmill Terrace there was a school dinners kitchen which prepared meals for several schools. Behind this was another site for the card school as was a place down beside the wee burnie.

We kids never took part in the gambling but it was an interesting spectator activity watching as significant sums, eg half crown or even five shillings, were won and lost. Players included regulars such as "The Snapper", Bob Galazzi, Tommy Glass, and a portly man called "Hully" (a Mr Hill).

A youth would be posted as a "sweeps" to look out for the police. I was never there when a raid took place but I heard of a case when the school was situated alongside the wee burnie and sweeps yelled "cops"! The cards and stakes were quickly gathered up in disorder and the school burst up in disarray with most players running across the field to the Dighty burn and into Fintry.

It was said poor Hully had some difficulty and was a comical sight in flight climbing through fences and across the burn.

As we grew into late boyhood we discovered Snooker. One had to be 14 years old to gain entry and our local saloon was "the

Maryfield" on Mains Loan. Despite what is said about snooker halls being dens of vice I found this not to be so. The Maryfield was owned by G. F. Brown , a Dundee bookmaker, and strictly run by two short middle aged men called John and Jim who both wore bonnets (flat caps) at all times. A table could be hired for two shillings per hour and cues and chalk provided. Crisps and lemonade were on sale.

There was a discipline about the hall enforced by Jim and John but also because there were usually older lads from our area who looked out for us. There was no violence that I saw and the game itself was played to the rules. It was after all "off the Street" in a heated environment with the interest of the game and if four were playing the cost was reasonable.

At weekends one could watch the money games. Strictly it was illegal to play for money but it went on nevertheless. Such games included "Life", "Continental", "Slosh" and "Golf".

A game of Life could have up to seven players and might be a noisy affair. Occasionally there would be a snooker tournament game of a district championship with visiting competitors. This was a respected event, held on table No1, and attracted much interest.

Early School days

In August 1945 I was enrolled in the infant school at Glenconner Drive Linlathen which was a ten minute walk from home. This was a Church of Scotland building pressed in to duty as a non-denominational school. My teacher was Miss Collie and the school headmistress was Miss Batchelor. The Lords prayer was said each morning before lessons but apart from that religion did not come into it, except for Easter and Christmas of course. There was no division on the basis of religion. The main hall of the building was split into classrooms by partitions and heated by gas powered heaters suspended from the ceiling. These heaters hissed as they heated and looked like flying saucers. Counting was taught using coloured card counters which were kept in sets in metal boxes which were, tantalisingly, ex sweet boxes. Writing was on slates with a slate pencil. Free milk was issued daily in small glass bottles with card tops which one pierced with a straw. Memories of the schooling are sparse but must have included medieval history stories as I distinctly remember a fascination with Mains castle and wondered if these knights and ladies occupied it at one time. Another item must have covered the skylark as I wandered off into the nearby field after school in search of one and saw one hovering above singing its sweet song. I must have achieved something as I received a school prize of a book about koala bear. I missed the prize-giving though as I was off on my first holiday, to Paignton, which would be in June 1947.

The school was still used for Church of Scotland services on Sunday and other community work after school hours. The Church offered a hand of friendship to German prisoners of war and on one occasion a group of PoWs passed through our room heading for a meeting in a committee room elsewhere in the school. The teacher warned us sternly not to look at them as they passed through the school, but I did anyway.

I caught the measles and was confined to bed for about two weeks.

I hated the confinement but I was given a small Meccano set which I enjoyed greatly. Playing with this small set started my interest in Engineering.

St Michaels Primary School

In August 1947 I was taken by my mother to enrol with many others at St Michaels Primary School in Graham Street inconveniently situated some three miles away. This was a large building of three blocks, terracotta brick greenish slate roof with a capacity of 1000 or so. It had been started in 1939 and the Northern block was still unfinished in 1947. The school had two distinct schools within it namely the non denominational (the Proddies) and the Catholics. Up to this time I was not aware that there such differences but the school system made it so. Each had their own curriculum and teachers and headmasters. It was a rather spartan and rough playground with much rough areas where air raid shelters had recently been removed. Having said that it was a good building of terracotta brick with airy classrooms, central heating with wash sinks and coat-hooks available at the entrances. There was a large assembly hall decorated at frieze level with paintings of romantic historical nature, knights and ladies again, but nice.

While at infant school my fellow pupils had come from my local area but now there was a wider catchment including Mid Craigie people. They were not so different from us, just strange. An odd thing about this school was that the children of the neighbourhood did not attend it only those living in Linlathen and Mid Craigie. This meant bussing four times per day as most went home for dinner (lunch). The morning buses left from Pitkerro drive and there was general melee to board them.

Generally girls went upstairs and boys down. This was enforced at 4pm home time as was segregation from the Catholic children. This led to loud singing of songs and if a catholic bus was passing there was a mutual rush to the windows to exclaim and receive derogatory remarks.

However apart from gender there was not any serious distinction made in the playground at times when both denominations shared the areas and there did not seem to be any discrimination or ill feeling that I was aware of.

My first teacher at St Michaels was Miss Wilson who was a short mature lady who stood no nonsense but was resigned and capable. The schoolroom was bare, Spartan and without decoration. The desks were standard school pattern i.e. two seater cast iron framed and rough pine woodwork and suitable size for 7 year olds. The floors were scrubbed pine and a faint odour of disinfectant pervaded the place. Jotters were supplied and kept at school and writing was by pencil; erasers were strictly not allowed. Sometimes a piano would be wheeled in for a music session, usually with singing.

There was a handwork lesson or two involving coloured squares of gummed paper. I remember an introduction to ancient Egyptian history so it must have appeared in a book we used.

Pupils were, reasonably, not allowed out of the school playground at interval times. However there was an illicit practice of sneaking out to the local shops to buy a bun or similar. A crusty small Vienna loaf was a favourite. I saw others at this and one day I tried it only to be caught red handed by Mr Doig the deputy head. The bread was confiscated and the belt was received. Lesson learnt, don't get caught.

The school did have its share of dishonest pupils who had even more dishonest friends. Things would be hawked around for sale by some of the tougher element. These were things that had been shoplifted or otherwise stolen but I did not know that.

I was offered an attractive ornamental badge-like disc for a penny and I bought the inoffensive article. That day there was a visit to the class by the headmaster who ordered all pockets to be emptied on to the desks. My disc was spotted along as was those of several others. The offence was noted and subsequently my mother was required to attend the school headmaster's room with me. It emerged that thieves had broken in to a firm called Mingware situated near Mid Craigie and made off with handfuls of their product. These items were then hawked round the school to unsuspecting youngsters. I received a dire warning that I must not buy such things which might be stolen goods. I suspect that my mother had made a robust defence based on the innocence of eight year olds.

The next year was taught by Miss Doren who was a younger woman and whose icy teaching did not get through to me. I took mumps during that year and was absent from school several weeks. On my return things had moved on but there was no attempt by the teacher to help me catch up. I fell behind and was left behind. The outstanding teacher we had was Mr McKell for, it seemed, two years; his class was fun and we learned many things.

He had us design and make puppets and this activity led to the formation of a puppet show. We gave performances at the City Art Gallery. In one play about a princess and a golden ball I played the part of the dragon complete with smoking breath provided by Mr McKell behind the scene via a rubber tube. This was education.

What was not education was our experience of English grammar analysis. It seems strange that such a subject was taught at primary school and what's more I hated it; mostly because I did not understand it. During our regular teachers absence we had the deputy head Mr Doig stand in and he was an analysis fanatic. That was one of the most unpleasant experiences of my primary school days. The final primary school years were taught by Mr Ford, a new teacher at that time who I was to meet later in life as the head teacher of my children's primary school. He had much mellowed by that time and seemed more reasonable. The Ford years were unremarkable and not as good as Mr McKell's. His style was strict and unfeeling with little creative educational activity. He did however once get us to take part in a play but I thought the organisation of this to be inept. English now included something called Synthesis and that was much more enjoyable altogether. Maybe Mr Ford was not so bad after all.

While "the Mikeys" was a rather basic school experience there were interesting things around the area if you looked. There was a high wall along the West boundary of the school and from the upper school rooms one could see into a scrapyard-like compound full of damaged army vehicles. These were vehicles ex-service which were being refurbished by the local Gray's garage on Clepington Road. These vehicles included lorries, vans, ambulances, pickups and even armoured cars. These wrecks could be seen being removed to the garage and emerging later refitted as bright as a new khaki pin.

A goods railway branch ran along the northern boundary of the school from Downfield goods yard on its way to the Maryfield goods yard and there was daily shunting of the yard with a steam locomotive. Maryfield yard received goods, supplies and coal by rail for Keillers' Mains Loan factory and various mineral dealers such as Taylor Brothers (coal and builders merchants). Steel was also a likely delivery to the Douglas foundry.

The school occupied a site on a high ridge running parallel to Clepington Road and afforded views to the south over the Tay valley and to the north to the farms of Emmock woods. There was therefore much to occupy the mind of a boy who yearned for the outdoors and enjoyed watching things going on around, but outside, the penitentiary-like school. Day-dreaming was an occupational hazard.

My father worked on the railway as a locomotive charge fitter at the Dundee West engine shed near Roseangle. One day he asked my brother Donald and I to bring our barrow (cartie) to Maryfield yard after school at about 5 pm. He had acquired scrap timber from repairs at the engine shed and had cut this into fence posts for his garden.

The posts were put on an engine known to be going to Maryfield when my father was coming off nightshift. It was getting dark when we got to Maryfield with my father and sure enough the engine was still there and about to return to Dundee engine shed. The posts were thrown down from the tender and we loaded them on to the cartie and brought the load home to Linlathen. Job done.

In 1948 my parents had their silver wedding. This was one of the rare house parties held. There was a requirement for extra seating and my mother had the offer of two long wooden seating forms from her friend Mrs Davidson who lived at the east end of Drumlanrig Drive in Mid Craigie, about a mile away. My brother and I were sent to pick up and carry these forms to our house. I remember this as a bruising tiring task. And we had to take them back a few days later.

The end of primary school was marked by the Qualifying examination ("qualy") which determined whether one went to an Academy or a Junior Secondary school.

This was strictly conducted and the results showed that I would be going to Stobswell Boys Junior Secondary. There had been discussion at home on my future and I was firmly in favour of a technical rather than an academic education. At Stobswell the main subjects were English, Maths, History and Geography, Technical, Science with Physical education and Music in addition.

Stobswell Junior Secondary School

Once again this school was built on the St Michaels pattern i.e. terracotta brick green slate roof three storeys, prison like.

Now the period system was to govern the school day of eight- 40 minute periods, 9am to 4 pm 5 days per week. There had evidently been streaming based on qualifying examination results and we in class 1A1 were told that if we opted to take French language and progress was good in the first 6 months the possibility of transfer to Morgan Academy might arise. I still preferred to stay at this Junior Secondary Technical School.

Those (very few) pupils who wished to do Commercial subjects rather than Technical could do so and this meant taking some classes at the Stobswell Girls School.

There was a strict regimented operating system at the School. The class was split into four houses and that determined where one sat in class. Movement to the next class was supervised in the corridors by teachers and, later as they were introduced, prefects. Anything gets dull if you are exposed to it day after day for months and years. However, relatively, I liked technical studies over academic studies and everything over Gym which was run by sadistic types in the main who seemed to think we were capable of Olympic style gymnastics. A half morning per week was spent at the sports field which was rather better and usually meant football at best and basketball at worst. Softball was a favourite of mine. If it rained hygiene lessons were given by an uncomfortable gym teacher.

The teaching staff were a mixed bunch. English and Maths teachers were usually graduate types and gowns were worn. History and Geography were often taught by the same teacher as gave English. Music was usually singing and was reasonably tolerable especially as the teacher Mr Murray ran a very tight ship with no nonsense.

Art classes, by Mr Jarvie, were mainly crayon drawing and water colour painting. The project I do remember was the design of a menu for a restaurant. I enjoyed doing that and received a good mark for it.

The school was reasonably well equipped especially in the technical department with new Harrison lathes, a shaper, vertical drills in the metalwork rooms and woodturning lathes in the woodwork rooms with proper benches and vices. The outstanding teacher here was Mr Fraser in metalwork. He had spent time in industry in real engineering and it showed. He would talk about examples of work in the outside world which I appreciated.

School was unremarkable in retrospect though adequate for the purpose. This was Junior Secondary education to Junior Leaving Certificate level and was described as a technical education. That was OK by me but there was a lack of any Heritage about the place. I would have valued a more cultural atmosphere rather than the functional bare surroundings of the place. The better teachers included Mr Kinnear (English, History and Geography), Mr Clark (Maths), Mr Fraser (Technical), the stern Mrs Campbell (Science).

Out of School- Part time work.

My mother pressed upon me the need to get an after school job as a message boy or paper boy. The paper delivery job was one my elder brother Donnie did and I had helped him on his round and did the job when he was away at the potato harvest or forestry work which they, at Morgan Academy, were allowed to do in senior years.

The newspaper business was run by Chae Stewart who was originally a Midmill Bleachfield worker who ran the papers business as a sideline. When the new shops were opened on Mauchline Avenue in Mid Craigie Chae took the lease of a shop full time and expanded the paper delivery business. The first of these rounds I experienced was the Mid Craigie round comprising Drumlanrig Drive and side Streets and Happyhillock and Craigie Mill houses. The second round I later helped with was Midmill Parkhead, Midmill Terrace, Bridgend and Fountainbleau. This latter round was more interesting and the people were generally friendlier. It was also an experience of an older way of life in old time buildings.

A typical day meant getting up to Mauchline Avenue for 6.30am and loading up with the morning papers. Mr Murray our next door neighbour also ran a newspaper business and the

25

distributor's lorry would drop off his papers at 6.30 when I would hitch a ride to Chae Stewarts which was the next drop. The papers were mainly Couriers, Daily Express and a few rarer titles such as the Noon Record (punter's paper), Daily Mail and Manchester Guardian. Not a Times, Scotsman or Glasgow Herald in sight. Comics included Dandy, Beano, Hotspur, Rover, Adventure, Eagle etc and adult weeklies such as People's Friend and My Weekly. One house even took the Psychic News. Fridays saw The Weekly News and The Reveille. A canvas bag was provided to carry the papers and could be quite heavy. I got to know how to fold a paper so that there were no frayed edges to tear in a letterbox. I also sensed poorer quality paper some days and better another even with the same title. Sundays could be hard work with Sunday Post, Sunday Pictorial, Reynolds News, The People, News of the World, Sunday Express, Sunday Mirror but no Sunday Times or Observer.

The nicer part of the Mid Craigie round was delivering to Happyhillock and Craigie Mill (otherwise "Snuff" Mill) houses. While the Mid Craigie houses were late 1930's brick built social housing Happyhillock was a stone built farm cottage house community with a south facing courtyard formed by the inside of the U. The inhabitants there seemed poorer than the average for the area and the water supply to these was by an outside standpipe. Sanitation did not appear to have reached Happyhillock evidenced by dry closet outhouses at some of the cottages. Happyhillock appeared to be a forgotten community but people did choose to live there perhaps because of the dire shortage of housing of any kind in the early 1950's. My impression was that some of the inhabitants were of tinker stock who had chosen to settle down. There was however a shop there run by a jovial Marty Crow. This was a small general store which also sold paraffin. When I was about seven or so I encountered a small girl there playing with a bottle with a liquid in it. She informed me that "There was a speeder in the paraffeen".

The area had a military presence in World War 2 and still present was an army van of the radio type. The field to the south east of Happyhillock had been an anti-aircraft rocket battery with many rows of rocket launchers waiting for the big raids that never came. Circa 1945 I was taken for a walk by my father along a path that ran from Happyhillock to Milton of Craigie Road along the backs of the houses in Drumlanrig Drive. The warlike rocket launchers were still there but in an abandoned state awaiting removal. I asked my dad why people had wars and he said it would be better if the politicians all got in a field and fought it out among themselves. That seemed reasonable to me.

Craigie Mill lay to the North of Happyhillock and comprised a ruined water driven mill building and surrounding houses and factory sheds. There were several good early Victorian managerial type houses and a long cottage row. I remember names like Masterton and Lumsden as residents of the better housing. We kids never knew this as Craigie Mill only as the "first ruins" or the Snuff mill. There was still a working textile presence in a group of converted cottages where bags were manufactured and reclaimed the proprietor being a Mr Foreman.

This marked the end of the paper round and I made my way homeward via Happyhillock Road and Parkhead Midmill.

The other paper round which I later stood-in delivering for Chae Stewart was Midmill and Fountainbleau Drive. The Dundee Bleachfield works at Midmill owned much of the land round the works which were situated at the bottom of the Pitkerro Road hill

27

leading to Longhaugh. The Dighty burn valley formed the base of the hill and was the reason for the location of the bleachworks.

The company owned two blocks of workers housing namely Midmill Terrace and Parkhead Midmill. They also owned the aforementioned Craigie Mill. The paper round started at Parkhead, then Midmill Terrace, then the boilerhouse of the bleachworks and Bridgend which was the name of the area just beyond the Dighty burn bridge. The round continued in the Linlathen housing estate via Fountainbleau Drive and Rowantree Crescent.

Parkhead was a west facing three storey tenement perpendicular to Pitkerro Road with two stair towers leading to platforms (pletties) on which the front doors were situated. These flats had indoor toilets and were probably of late 19th century construction. Some of the ground floor flats were of a superior nature probably for foreman or junior management grade. There were gardens out the back and a washhouse on Happyhillock Road. Names I remember are Stewart, Duncan, Whitehead, Dunbar, and Dargie. There was a weatherboard shop alongside the Parkhead building near Pitkerro Road run by Ina Lowrie and this was also the local shop for my neighbourhood. A curious occurrence was at the twice daily teabreak when a parade of workers would briskly walk up from the works to their home for presumably a light snack.

Midmill Terrace was situated some 250 yards down Pitkerro Road from Parkhead on the right and parallel to it, and was an earlier construction of two storeys and garrets. It was set back from Pitkerro Road by a wall and their garden plots. On the other side of the building there were a number of stair towers leading to the first floor flats and inside stairs leading to the garrets. Beyond were drying greens and a long row of toilet

28

outhouses backing on to the boundary wall. A washhouse was situated at the entry to the terrace to serve the many households. Names I remember from the terrace were Flood, Heffron, McLeod and Masterton.

The paper round started at Parkhead and then Midmill Terrace. After the terrace a visit was made inside the bleachworks to the fireman. This was a welcome visit as the boilerhouse was warm and contained large coal fired Lancashire type boilers. The fireman would acknowledge the delivery and say he was now going home for breakfast. Next was Bridgend which was a small group of houses over the Dichty bridge at the bottom of the hill. There was a larger villa, probably a management house (Cunningham?) and two sets of cottages. In one of these cottages lived an ancient gentle couple, the old lady being quite bent. Any dealings I had with her were pleasant. Their cottage had an end portion in which ponies were kept. In autumn an old apple tree there yielded sweet small yellow apples.

There was another villa to the right with a higher position which I believe was called Longhaugh house. This was the one time residence of the Bleachfield manager.

I found the Bleachfield community to be an agreeable one.

I then continued the round proceeding to Fountainbleau Drive on the Linlathen housing estate. I learned later that the grand name was taken from Fountainbleau farm which occupied the ground in the area prior to the building of Linlathen. The rest of the round was unremarkable except for a customer in Rowantree Crescent who constantly complained of the papers delivery being late. Strangely they took two Couriers; but I knew that the brothers in the house fought like cat and dog.

The paper rounds were temporary jobs in which I was standing in for my brother Donald when he was off on breaks from school e.g. Forestry commission working holidays. I did other message boy jobs the first of which was when I was just 13 years of age. My mother got me to take a message boy job at Dundee Eastern Cooperative Society (DECS) (the "Sosh") branch at Forfar Road.

The "Message boy" jobs.

This was the standard type of large co-op grocery store which served most grocery and butcher's items. Customers would enter the store and place their membership book in a vertical box then take a bentwood seat. A serving assistant when free would take the next book in the queue and call out the name. The customer then went to the counter at which the assistant worked and asked for the required items which were then fetched by the assistant. The customer then paid for the order or had it "put on the book". This could be paid for once per week or when funds were available. Hardware, furniture, ironmongery, electrical and clothing goods could also be purchased from the DECS central branch in the Seagate on production of the book. This was a credit system which was watched by the store manager and if balances were building up and no payments made a message would be sent to the customer to "see the manager".

The store assistants wore brown overall coats, the assistant manager a grey coat and the manager a white coat. Exceptionally "M" the orders assistant wore a black coat. The lowest form of life was the message boy. One of the lady assistants was Betty Murdoch who was to become Dundee's leading ballroom dancer who along with her husband Bob Barty became Scottish Ballroom dancing champions. This was an after school and Saturday job and the main task was to pick up a box of groceries load up the message bike and deliver the goods to the customer's house.

These loads could be heavy and I regularly pedalled up Mains Loan standing with all my weight on the pedals till I had to dismount and push up the interminable hill.

Most of the deliveries were in the Maryfield area but could be further away e.g. Arbroath Road Gotterstone farm cottages. The message boys came under the control of the black coated assistant M. He was a middle aged grumpy man who kept us on our toes. His going home clothes included an Antony Eden hat and a rolled umbrella. If there were no orders ready the floor had to be brushed or a shelf tidied and all of this for just 10 shillings per week.(50p)

The message bikes were wrecks with doubtful brakes and worn tyres. If a puncture occurred you had to fix it yourself. However when a bike became dilapidated it was sent to "The Bakery" for overhaul. This bakery was the central bakery for all DECS shops and was situated on Clepington Road. It even had its own railway siding on the Maryfield goods line which ran along the back. One day on turning up for work I was peremptorily told by M to take a given bike to the bakery for overhaul. It seemed a long way to go but at least it was empty. I cycled along Clepington Road and found the hallowed Bakery and after a few queries got to the bike repair man. There was no bus fare provided for the return journey so I set off to walk back to Forfar Road DECS.

After what seemed a very long walk I arrived tired at the store and was immediately asked by M where I had been. It did not seem to matter that he had sent me on this errand and did not provide bus fare for the return. This was however typical of the unjust management style of M. One nail in the coffin of this job.

I noticed that it was rarely ordinary people's houses I delivered to but mainly middle class people in villas or "good" tenement addresses. These were the types who thought nothing of dropping off their message list for delivery or phoning in their order. I never actually experienced the alleged demand at four o-clock for "two ounces of boiled ham to be sent up for teatime" but it was believable.

If the job was boring, tedious and heavy there was however the chance to experience every day shop life including the firmly girdled middle aged serving lady who asked me to pick up a heavy tin from a lower shelf as "if I do it something is liable to snap". A grocer patting a butter portion or slicing cheese was a work of art. Other unusual errands I was sent on included a message to the occupant of the flat above the store to remind him that rent was overdue and a message for my own mother to see the manager about the "back of the book". The back of the book was the credit system and clearly a debt was building up which he wished reduced.

One factor which kept customers at DECS was the dividend system which provided a lump sum once per year to members. This could be about 10% and was once as high as 12.5%. And then of course there was the credit system.

My DECS job was unremarkable otherwise and when potato harvest time approached I asked the shop manager to be excused for the three weeks. The white coated manager looked unhappy with this request and refused my request suggesting that if I did not want his (wonderful) job I would have to go. So I went.

A year or so later the other after (and before) school job I had was with Grewar's the butcher in Albert Street. This required being at the shop by 7.30 am to load the bike and start the round.

Here the bike was nearly new but the round was long. It included Taybank, Craigiebank, Baxter Park Terrace, Bingham Terrace and odd outlying addresses in Craigie Drive or rural Arbroath Road. The pay was better (18 shillings per week) and there was a perk on Saturday of a few slices of Lorne sausage and two slices of black pudding. A butchers shop is a very busy place and has to be kept clean. Jimmy Grewar would inspect the message boys and send them to wash their hands.

There was no back shop, rather a basement where the butcher would descend or emerge through the open trapdoor as if by magic to the workroom below; on the run. The basement included a sausage making bench, stores, a boiler for making meat loaf and other products, the cold room being in the main shop. The butcher was Jimmy Grewar and his assistant Jimmy Reilly. The sides of meat would hang on hooks (to drip) on the left on entry to the shop the counter being on the right and sawdust on the floor. I was one of two message boys and there was also a van delivery to further flung and commercial customers for example the Wallace Foundry (Dura Street) canteen. Jimmy Reilly did these deliveries using Jimmy Grewar's Hillman Husky based van.

The job involved six mornings per week and five afternoons with alternate Saturday afternoon working. Jimmy Grewar was fair in the main but the customer was always right even if in the wrong. I delivered a parcel of meat to a house in Bingham terrace with instruction to not ring the bell but leave the parcel on the back window sill. The customer let his dog out at breakfast time and the dog got the parcel and I got a telling off for it.

Hygiene was paramount in this job and there was a fingernail inspection daily before work. Fair enough. I dreaded the cleaning up we had to help with at end of day as JG would insist on us being there till right on six o'clock sweeping up the sawdust, polishing the brass weights with whitening and such chores.

The early hours were proving a problem and the job was making inroads to my time so when the potato harvest again came round I gladly resigned that job.

Other Friendships

My other activities at this time varied depending on who I was getting along with, and where I was living. I was at times living with my sister Rena whose husband had to travel with his job and I was detailed to live at Stobswell Road to run messages and generally help.

I built up a friendship with some of the Catherine Street kids of my age and in summer there was a daily morning game of football at Baxter Park.

When home at Linlathen my friendships were varied and changeable usually when a disagreement occurred. At my first potato harvest in 1953 I met some lads from Baldovie which is a country area to the north east of Dundee. Dave Edgar lived on a smallholding there with his Grandfather "Auld Geordie" his long distance driver father (for Vidor Ltd) and his younger brother Douglas.

Dave's mother had died of cancer and his Aunt Lilas Miller attended as housekeeper. Dave's cousin Doug Miller was her son.

I found the Baldovie Toll area an idyllic place with trees and a curling pond and old bridge over the Fithie burn. The smallholding was one of those set up by the Department of Agriculture in the 1930's and comprised a bungalow a barn and six acres of farmland on which market garden crops were grown in addition to hens and a piggery. The surroundings at Baldovie were lovely with trees, a burn ("the sweet Burn" or Murroes burn) and a crossroads at Baldovie Toll. The holding was situated on the Newbigging Road to the south of the Pitkerro house (or castle) estate. The ornate lodgehouse was almost opposite the holding on the drive to the big house which dates from the 16th century..

Dave's cousin Doug Miller lived at Pitkerro house in a flat over the stables his mother being Dave Edgar's Auntie Lilas.

I helped out at the holding preparing raspberry canes, boiling potatoes for the pigs, assisting with sawing logs and also potato lifting. There was an old Fordson tractor which was fun to help with and sometimes drive. It started on petrol but was switched to run on paraffin when heated up. Starting was by handle and we usually stood on the handle as it was a heavy engine to turn over (not a good idea but it never backfired). Gear change was done stationary as the clutch pedal was also the footbrake. On one occasion we transported two pigs in the holding small trailer from the holding up to Pitkerro house stables where there was a pig pen. We found Doug in a small outhouse boiling up some potatoes for his pigs. Pigs were fed on the small potatoes, called chats, arising from the potato dressing or grading operation. Leisure time at Baldovie was spent hanging out in the barn, going to the cinema in Broughty Ferry, the Reres in Gray Street, or running around on our bikes.

Early one idyllic summer evening Dave got a call from a friend called Swan to say that he was exercising a horse and cart for his father and would be calling by Baldovie. The Swan family ran a greengrocer business from their smallholding at Emmock Woods where Dave Edgar's Uncle Dave Fowler also had a smallholding. We were invited to join young Swan on the flat cart and we took our bikes for the return journey. It was a lovely experience moving effortlessly and sedately through the countryside singing along and calling out to any young females we passed on the way. The route was by way of Baldovie Toll to Ballumbie farm then Duntrune, Barns of Wedderburn, Middleton farm and Powrie thence to the holding at Emmock woods. After a short stay at Emmock we returned to Baldovie on our bikes, mainly downhill.

In my mid-teens my friend and neighbour Benny Murray had also joined the Baldovie group. One early summer day we planned to have a Sunday cycle tour to Forfar to visit the Pavilion Cinema there. Bennie had to finish his Sunday paper round and after Sunday lunch we biked out to Baldovie to meet Doug Miller. Dave did not join us due to work commitments. It was a lovely day as we set off up the Road to Kellas and Bucklershead taking the side Road to Carrot hill. After a breather at Carrot it was downhill to Kinnetles and on to the Forfar Road. We arrived downhill into Forfar by 3.30 and thought about a place to leave the bikes while we had tea and attended the cinema.

I had visited relations in Green St. Forfar while holidaying at Glamis the previous year. This was Wullie Horsburgh, my mother's cousin, and his wife Ede and family. I knocked on the door which was answered by the son Peter and introduced myself and asked if we could leave our bikes round the back. Ede came to the door and made us most welcome and was happy to allow us to leave the bikes. I thanked her and said we were off to get something for tea in the town before the cinema. She would not hear of this and offered us a meal which we accepted gratefully. We enjoyed our steak pie and potatoes followed by cake and tea. Ede's daughter Betty arrived in from work where she was a conductress on Alexander's buses.

We went off to the Pavilion Cinema which was two hundred yards away in Queen St and enjoyed the show. The bikes were picked up quietly and we set off up Forfar High Street to Dundee Loan and South to the Main Forfar Road. It was dark and the hill was steep but we ploughed on to the summit at Petter Den and from there downhill to Tealing and Murroes. Doug left us at Duntrune and Bennie and I continued home via Barns of Wedderburn and Longhaugh completing a great day out.

Another trip took place in my 16th year on or about the first Monday of the Dundee Holiday week which would be late July. I met two neighbourhood friends Johnny Haxton and George Flood one morning and they asked if I wished to join them on a bus trip to Kirriemuir which lies northwest of Forfar. They had friends there at the berry-picking. We boarded the Alexander country bus at Midmill which ran through to Kirremuir via Murroes. This was a nice tour of the verdant Angus countyside and we duly arrived at the square in Kirriemuir. There was a nice Franchi cafe there where we had a pie and a soft drink or coffee. Upstairs in this cafe there was a billiard saloon and we repaired there for a pleasant afternoon frame or two. The lads then said it was time to visit the friends at berryfields outside Kirrie. This was a pleasant walk out to a farm where there were huts for the resident pickers. It was not unusual for families to decamp from the city to spend a working holiday on these fruit farms. I noted some tent like camping of an ancient looking sort formed from bent limbs of bushes. These I was told were tinker type tents.

We visited the pickers huts and the lads were welcomed by their friends. This was a mother and several daughters and their friends. It was decided to walk in to Kirrie to a cafe for the evening. It came out in discussion that the lads were planning to stay the night in the hut. Now I had formed an opinion about the hospitable pickers and their basic accommodations but kept these thoughts to myself. They were a pleasant enough crowd and the evening passed in convivial banter. As we were sitting in the cafe I noticed a bus sitting with 'Dundee Via Forfar' on its indicator which surprised me as I thought the last bus had gone. I got up and walked out and boarded the bus and eventually got home to sleep in my own bed. It was a pleasant and memorable day out but I was not prepared for roughing it in a berryfield hut.

This was a time when I was hanging out with the local lads centred on Midmill terrace. We would meet there before going on to a cinema or snooker evening. A rare and memorable event occurred one early evening when a local lad called 'Swift' turned up at Midmill on his bike with a piano accordion strapped to his back. He sat down on a bank and started to play wonderful Scottish music. Time seemed to stop as people came to halt and enjoyed this impromptu concert. This surprising talent and the summer evening made it a enjoyable experience.

The Tatties

School in general seemed to be, and was, an artificial environment which I did not like so when in second year the potato harvest happened I was in my element.

It was the practice at the time to allow schoolchildren to attend the potato harvest to pick the potatoes. This was a hangover from wartime scarcity of labour. Pupils could opt out and attend school as normal or join in the harvest. There were two harvest options viz Education department scheme or private. The Education authority scheme meant turning up at school early, say 7.15 am and boarding buses for transport to the farms. Meals were provided near the farm usually in a country school.

The private scheme involved approaching your farmer of choice and asking him to apply for your private permit. The private scheme paid better and was more convenient for me but no buses and no mid-day meal.

My friends and I went to Maclean's farm at Ballumbie and submitted our names and addresses. Surprisingly the private permit turned up at the school so all was set for the "tatties". We were picked up at Midmill by a Macleans Albion lorry already carrying other pickers about 7.20am and taken to Ballumbie farm. The potato field was paced out by the foreman (gaffer) and whinbush (Broom) branches marked the allocated length, or "bit" to be picked by an individual picker. The potatoes were dug up by an Oliver elevator harvester which laid the potatoes in a line. The picker's job was to pick these into a basket, or "scull", which was lifted by a man into a following cart. The pace of work was set by the speed of the digger and it could be a rush to get your bit lifted before the cart arrived. It was gritty work but the squad bent to the task and there was little nonsense. On some farms an unloved scatterer harvester was used which spread the potatoes over a wider area and took more work. The fresh air, cold and manual work did something to the person. It was part of growing up, working to a pace and getting fit while meeting a requirement. The plum job was to be "on the cart" which involved standing on the moving cart emptying the baskets being thrown up by the man and in turn throwing the empty basket back to the ground. This cart job was shared out so it paid to be in the gaffer's good books.

This was the first full day's manual work I had done and I was so tired at the end of the first few days that I lay down after tea and immediately fell asleep.

Ballumbie farm was the W&A McLean base farm situated on the Road from Chae Mollison's smiddy on the Drumgieth Rd to Duntrune. The Ballumbie fields were lifted first and then the picking squad moved on to other fields let for McLean crop. So the next farm for us was Stotfauds near Monikie. These fields were very large and exposed to cold wind. The harvesting equipment, operated by the farmer of Stotfauds, was basic being the scatterer type pulled by an old Ford tractor and there were two diggers and two carts operating. This was hard going and monotonous only broken mid-morning for a piece (midser). The farmer was very strict and pickers were not allowed near the steading for lunch break (mid-lousing). We were glad to see the end of that large field. Next was cauld Carmyllie a high and even colder farm but at least there were trees and more modern harvesting machinery ie the Oliver elevator which laid the crop in a straight row. There was an old quarry next to the field, Carmyllie had many quarries, which legend had it contained a tractor which had gone over the cliff like edge into the green depths below. We were however allowed to use the barn for our mid-day break. I noticed that the farm workers' housing on this farm was poor, old and very basic, the children seemed to be in rags.

I got to know the people at Ballumbie farm. The boss was Dougal Maclean, who drove a large McLoughlin Buick limousine, but the day to day running of the farm business was in the hands of Chic Maclean in his Singer saloon and Ron Maclean in a Land Rover. The younger Doug McLean (Ford 8 1938) worked as a tractorman on the farm. Graham Maclean was still at school. The Maclean business included a potato merchanting business and they hired fields beyond Ballumbie for potato crop.

Ballumbie was all mechanised by this time with 3-Ferguson tractors a D2 Caterpillar and a Nuffield. The grieve was Eck and the workers included Jock Cumming, his father, Arthur Taylor and a cattleman. Ernie, an ex German POW with "Egypt" tattooed on his arm also worked there.

I enjoyed the potato harvest experience greatly and was sad to be returning to the school routine.

Another task which I had to do when about 14 years old was to go to my Grandmother's house in Salem St. after school on Thursdays to get her groceries in from the DECS shop at West Port which was about half a mile away and I was told to insist on being served by Albert. Her house was an old cottage with an equally old interior which I would describe as Victorian. There was a black coal "range", no electricity and lighting was by gas. My tasks included going for the groceries, taking out the ashes and rubbish to the bin and also going to the butcher and to the paraffin shop. The "paraffin and stick" shop was in Dudhope Crescent Road and was run by two older ladies. It was a remnant of the time when many houses had oil lamps and nearly everyone burnt coal for heating.

My grandmother was an old lady, somewhat crotchety and seemed to be always in a bad mood. The strange thing is that there was a DECS shop at the end of her lane but she did not favour it for some reason. I would sometimes be sent back with something to a shop because it was the wrong variant that I had not been forewarned of. I was sent down to the DECS main shop in Seagate for a "flue brush" which the assistants there had never heard of.

I was late getting to Salem lane one day because I was held up at school and my grandmother was not there. She had gone for the groceries herself and I was not asked back.

School was unremarkable in retrospect though adequate for the purpose of a Junior Secondary leaving certificate. That was fine by me but I would have valued a place with more heritage.

The end of secondary school was a happy time and on the last day I walked out without ceremony or regret.

The next stage of my life was approaching and my uncle Doug Shepherd had arranged for me to have an interview for an engineering apprenticeship at the Caledon Shipyard Dundee.

Family Holidays

My father's job with the Railway had the perk of a free pass to anywhere in the UK. This meant that we had an annual family holiday for a week. This was unusual in the area as few families had a holiday away at that time.

The first holiday I remember was in 1947 to Paignton in Devon. My father's pass allowed travel on the LMS only so routing via LMS and associated companies was necessary. We travelled to Perth and changed to an overnight train to Birmingham.

A wait was required there for a train to Paignton. Paignton was still in a wartime emergency state as far as facilities were concerned. This meant few Street lights, dowdy surroundings, nothing in the shops with parks and local amenities in a run-down state. But the sands had been cleared and therefore the seaside was available.

The next year we went to Lowestoft in Suffolk. The routing was less problematic because British Railways had been formed and we could use the LNER and other routes. Lowestoft was in recovery from the war with several bombsites all round.

Again the seaside had recovered before much else and as I remember the weather was kind to us. We holidayed in boarding houses and "rooms and service "was the deal. This meant that my mother got the groceries required and these were cooked by the landlady. Food rationing was in force of course so we were limited to our usual ration allotment. Lowestoft was a fishing town so our diet was supplemented by fresh local catch.

Hastings was next and that involved travelling via London thence by Southern railway to Hastings on the South East coast of England. I had my first experience of the London tube which seemed frightening yet exhilarating. The fare from Kings Cross to Charing Cross was about 6 pence. We breakfasted, travel was always overnight, in the ABC café where ham and eggs were available off the ration.

Our family party on this holiday comprised my parents, younger sister Nancy, my next older brother Donnie and, unusually, my elder brother Robert who had just returned from National Service in the Royal Navy.

Hastings is a historic town and visits were made to nearby places such as Rye and Battle. There was a coastal walk along the cliffs which included viewing a downed V1 flying bomb in a makeshift museum.

In a subsequent year we visited London somewhere in the East end near Liverpool Street station. We travelled as usual overnight on the Friday evening train from Dundee direct to London. Kings Cross station was a bustling terminus and was black as night with the blacked out rooflights and the accumulated

43

grime of a hundred years of steam power. However light was permeating through a smoky haze from the great semi-circular glass frontage of the station on to the magnificent sight of our motive power into London in the shape of a great green A4 Pacific locomotive with the, to me, bizarre sight of a negro fireman trimming the tender coal. It must have been 1951 because we visited the Festival of Britain. This was a great experience because everything was new and up-beat. While London was re-building after the war there were a large number of bomb sites around.

Visits were made to the Tower of London and the Thames environs including a river trip from Westminster to Woolwich from where we crossed on the Woolwich Ferry steamboat and visited some of the haunts of my father's childhood in North Woolwich. The Thames at the time was a heavily polluted river and I recall the water surface at Woolwich pier being thick with a black scum of, probably, soot.

We returned to London the next year on the invitation of Rose (Anderson), a distant cousin of my father, who lived at Shooter's Hill Woolwich. Her flat was high on the hill and looked West to the distant city with Battersea Power station "like an upturned kitchen table". Rose lived in a flat in a shared tall Victorian terrace house on Shooters Hill. Her house in Woolwich had been destroyed in the war and her husband killed at his work due to bombing of Henley's cable factory.

Weymouth in Dorset was the next year's holiday destination and things were looking up with flower beds and well maintained parks and gardens. Our train from Waterloo was hauled by double headed Bulleid Pacific steam locomotives which were a great sight especially when their driving wheels lost traction and spun till the sanding gear allowed traction to be resumed. That summer was especially hot, some lineside fields were on fire and the exposure at the seaside led to my suffering badly sunburned skin.

The following year we travelled to Gorleston in Norfolk to holiday in a chalet. This was different and had more freedom than boarding house accommodation. We experienced the Broads and Great Yarmouth with its seemingly large funfair.

Then there was Cornwall where we boarded with the Tucker family. My father believed in getting value for money travel as Cornwall was about as far as one could travel by rail from Dundee. St Austell was the centre of the China Clay industry and great white pyramids formed the landscape.

The local dialect was wonderful and there were trips to Newquay and Fowey. We travelled for the first time by the Great Western Region of BR and experienced the wonderful Kings and Castles locomotives of that line with their gleaming brasswork on funnel and safety valves.

Subsequent holidays included a return to Weymouth, then to Bigbury in Devon which would be the last of the family holidays as I remember them. I was approaching mid-teens and did not wish that kind of holiday. I would prefer to attend the fruit picking of the Dundee area or join in the family holidays of my sisters who usually had camping or farm based holidays locally.

Jane U. Shepherd Middleton

Robert S. Middleton

DM with Aeroplane 1943

Ella and Ginger 1943

DM and Rena Linlathen 1947

DM and Donnie Murraygate 1948

Doon Terrace People 1955

St Michaels School Dundee   (photo D C Thomson)

See image credits p267

Dundee East and Drumgeith

St Michaels Primary circa 1950, teacher Mr McKell

Part 2 1956-1961

Pre-Apprenticeship

"Your uncle has arranged an interview for you at the shipyard and you are expected there at 4.30 on Monday" my mother said as I arrived in from Stobswell School. I had known for some time that I wanted "to be an engineer" and it had only been a matter of deciding where at and doing what. I had discussed large marine engines with my father who was a locomotive fitter with the railway and this planted a seed of interest. There was a family background in seagoing engineering with marine engineer uncle Bob Donald lost in a torpedo attack in 1940 while serving as second engineer officer on an iron ore carrier the SS FISCUS. My main mentor however had been my sister Rena and her husband Gerd Bueckardt who had spent the war years as a ship's engineer (Kriegsmarine) and who had encouraged me in my technical education at school and did not hesitate to discuss technical problems. When I was aged 12 Rena gave me, as a Christmas present, the book "Engines for Power and Speed" by F.E. Dean. This book was fundamental in encouraging me to become an engineer. It also demonstrates that Rena did not underestimate the ability of a young person to appreciate such a book.

My own idea of an engineer was as some kind of technician who dealt with the mysteries and complexities of the world and ship's engineering seemed a closed system which one could begin to understand. I had been fascinated by the sheer size of marine engines and wanted to work with them.

So that was settled and although the employment prospect had not overly worried me it was with a feeling of settled comfort that

I made my way to the Caledon Stannergate Shipyard for the interview with Mr David Kydd the yard training officer. This was to be my first encounter with "the lodge" that is the porter's office at the yard official entrance. All who entered had to pass here and the lodge man was a Jimmy Brownlee who was an ex Scotland goalkeeper of considerable repute in the town and who was shown great respect, or else!

And here too was the first encounter with engineering hardware in the shape of an enormous valve of the type used in engine-rooms and presumably used here in connection with the office building heating system or yard water supply. "To the training officer lad" he indicated and in his kindly way directed the green youth to an office across the yard just inside the main gate.

The training officer's quarters must surely have been an air raid bunker for wartime as it was windowless, semi-circular in section, and constructed entirely of steel with protruding rivet heads similar to ship construction. I sat down and waited in the semi-circular, mini-nissen hut shaped waiting room and presently the training officer opened his office door, looked out over his glasses asking "Yes"?

The budding trainee explained his presence and a short interview followed in which my future was discussed. I was then directed to go to the ambulance room in the adjacent building for the "medical" a rite which I anticipated with some trepidation and associated with the process experienced by my acquaintances before induction to national service. I found that I was in the company of some eight chaps in the same situation and the preliminary measurements of height weight and date of birth were taken. The "preliminary" feeling arose from the certainty of the "drop the trousers bit" which was characteristic of all such

52

medicals and presumably was a check that one had not been suffering rupture prior to joining the yard.

That over, a short interview with the Engineering manager came next. The "outside" Marine Engineering Department's managers occupied an office in a two floor wooden building to the east of the main yard gate. These Caledon managers supervised the engineering work in progress on ships building. The details of one's application form were sifted by the assistant marine engineering manager, Mr Anderson, while the manager himself, Mr Kerr, looked over his spectacles from the drawing before him only occasionally to peer disdainfully at the specimen being interviewed. "You have model engineering as a hobby; have you ever made anything?" the assistant asked. "I have made a boiler sir, and I bought a small engine." "Did it work?" "Yes sir" and that was that. "We'll be in touch " Mr Anderson said and I left the office of the seemingly temporary building at the left side of the main gate.

The evening was one of those in early autumn of still air with a golden sky at 5pm and as I climbed the footpath to the Ferry Road for a bus home I wondered what it would be like to work in this great steel workshop. The yard had a smell of its own compounded of rusting steel, coal fires, bitumen refining at Briggs next door and the smell of the river and, as I would find in time, specialist smells depending on the part of the yard or ship one was in and its state of construction.

I received a letter within a week informing me that I had been accepted for employment and that a "boys" job would precede my actual apprenticeship. There were many such pre-apprenticeship positions which required to be filled servicing the various offices and lodges mainly in a messenger capacity but including store boys, and in retrospect the best job, print room boys.

This then was my introduction to the shipyard scene and after New Year the job would begin, hopefully, a 50 year working phase of my existence. I was glad that schooldays were nearing their end as they had never been really enjoyable but had supplied the basic language and number skills necessary for the tradesmen of tomorrow. Without ceremony or regret I left school one Friday in December 1955 and never looked back, except to return a book on engines which I had forgotten to return to the school library.

When word got round that I was starting at the yard I found new comrades in the workers of the locality. I had seen since childhood days the dark clothed figures of the yard workers passing in their way home and they had about them a basic masculinity associated with hard work in an outside environment. The yard had always had its special buses and routes for its workers and the yard men walked with a swagger and pride similar to the North East miners' attitude.

There were therefore no misgivings in my heart in contemplation of the working life. The brief potato harvesting working periods in my early teens had allowed a taste of manual labour to be experienced and had been fun.

The only detail to be faced was to collect an insurance card from the "Broo" in Gellatly Street and report to the Boilershop drawing office on the first day with my National Insurance card, better known as the "books".

Print Boy Marine Engineering Department (MED)

My Instructions were to report at 8.45 am on 5th January 1956 to the MED offices at the Caledon Boilershop to serve as a print room assistant, better known simply as a "print boy". This was to be my workplace for some 8 months but at the age of 15 it seemed a considerable time. The building comprised a generally curved fronted redbrick structure, on the North end gable of the Boilershop with the curved office building lower left (page 130). The chimney stack was for the plate furnace in the Boilershop), having the engineering drawing office on the upper floor and the Boilershop lodge, ambulance room and drawing store on the ground floor. This building connected to the large two bay corrugated sheeted shed forming the Boilershop typical of many Engine and Boilershops in the country. The upper floor offices provided the accommodation for the administration and drawing offices of the Marine Engineering department the function of which was the design of the engine-room, propulsion, funnel and boiler-room equipment on board ships to be built at the yard.

My first problem was to find the print room and I reported to the "lodge". The lodge-keeper directed me to the print room on the first floor and I climbed the stairs to find it. The door to the print room gave off a landing at the top of the stairs and on entering it I found the room lit only by an overhead skylight and artificial light. The room, a dull unwelcoming place with a slightly acrid smell, contained the necessary equipment for the production of blueprints and whiteprints for the various marine engineering workshops of the yard and Boilershop. The room was brick built and painted a cream colour with a skylight in the roof but no other windows. There was a large table with a steel edge for trimming the drawing prints. Two cupboards one built in, i.e. a "press", and the other a wooden structure. The sink was brick built and lead lined to resist the chemicals mixed there. The centre of the room was occupied by the Halden printing machine in which drawings over light sensitive paper were exposed to a strong light prior to the developing stage. There was an ammonia developing machine for making white prints and a roller machine for developing blueprints. A large clothes horse hung from the roof for drying the developed prints. A door in this room led through to the engineering estimators' room and their staff would pass through regularly.

I took in this sight and a few minutes later a lad entered the room. He introduced himself as Jim Horrocks from Rockwell school, also a new start that morning. He was a medium height chap with thick glasses and an attempt at a Tony Curtis haircut. However far from presenting a bookish impression Jim put himself over as a hard man with glasses. He did not say very much but went through the usual discomfort that people suffer on first encounter with another in unfamiliar surroundings. Some discussion followed about the things familiar such as what school, what apprenticeship and where in town one came from.

Enter Wullie Martin "the print man". He was to be our immediate gaffer for the duration, 5ft 7, forty five plus-ish, fag in mouth, stubble, balding with strands, Daily Record under his arm, smart but round shouldered walk. "You will be the new boys eh?, nods, "yes, good morning". "Right let's get the machines on then" he said and pulled the main switch for the printing equipment. First the Halden printing machine sprung to life with its fabric bands moving round and round ready to carry the drawing and light sensitive paper together against the glass semi cylinder behind which the brilliant lights shone. This machine ran all the working day except lunchtime and was one of those which had to be left running for 15 minutes after the lights had been switched off to dissipate the heat from the glass. It gave off a smell of toasted textile fabric.

"Now for breakfast and a shave" says Wullie. "Take the tea can over to Boab's and get it filled,that will be 2d. Also get me a ham (bacon) roll, 6d. Boabs is the transport shack just across the railway lines". I took the first duty; Jim put the electric kettle on for Wullie's shave.

Boab's was a snack joint in which tea, rolls, etc were prepared for drivers and others using the docks or working there. He, with fag in mouth, filled the tea-can and prepared the roll for Wullie's breakfast first removing a wad of soft bread from its interior. A great pile of such wads was present on his counter. His hut provided bench seating accommodation for the normal customers and there was usually a lively crowd in for the morning 9.00am break, starting time being 7.30 for most workers. These were usually lorry drivers, Caledon workers in transit from Boilershop to yard, workers from Pattullo and Barr potato merchants or the ICI fittings works, dockers and railway shunters. This was not a very big place seating perhaps 15 people on benches round the wall and most of the business was take-away. Occasionally the hut rumbled and shook as a goods train slowly passed close by along the docks railway. The docks railway for goods trains to the docks and power station ran between the hut and our office and often one had to wait while a train slowly passed.

Back in the print room a newly shaved Wullie has the Record under scrutiny through a cloud of eye watering smoke. The roll and tea are consumed and the lads are informed that they may have some tea if they pay a share of the cost. It should be mentioned here that the print room trio were not invited to join in the drawing office tea school which was run by the secretaries. Wullie followed the hourly paid trades in having a nine oclock tea-break while the office workers had a ten o'clock break.

Breakfast over, the group turned their attention to the business of the day. A sheaf of original drawings awaited printing and distribution to the various workshops. Original drawings were produced by the Engineering draughtsmen on semi transparent tracing paper in order that prints could be made by light transmission on to sensitive paper

Prints from these drawings were issued to a limited number of people as preliminary drawings or for early stages of ship construction. When fully finished the drawings would be traced in black ink on to a blue coloured translucent linen by girl tracers and would form a very permanent record.

The lads were made aware by Wullie of the value of the drawings one of which could represent 4 months or more of a senior draughtsman's time and therefore the embedded value was significant.

The exposing process comprised feeding the roll of translucent drawing into the Halden machine together with the roll of sensitive paper rather like feeding a wringer forty two inches wide but the drawing had to be very parallel or the drawing would "run off" especially if a long drawing was involved.

The type of sensitive paper used was chosen depending on whether a blueprint or a white print was required.

Blueprints i.e. white lines on a blue ground and tough paper were used for workshops and fitting out foremen while white prints, dark blue lines on a white ground and thinner paper, were used for office based managers and estimators.

The first print Wullie was to make as a demonstration for us was a blueprint and appropriate paper was selected and the Halden exposer swallowed up drawing and sensitive paper. The exposed print was then taken to the blueprint developer which would essentially wet the paper via rollers with first one chemical (developer) then another (fixer), the print being carried up by hand to the drying hanger or horse; thus a blueprint was made.

The drawings could be up to 12 feet in length and either 30" or 40" wide so the print room really became draped in blue if a big run was on.

After the drawings had been produced and dried they had to be trimmed so that the edges would be clean and parallel to the drawing borders. The process of trimming was carried out using a razor blade cutting along the straight edge attached to the trimming table. This job required much more skill than was at first apparent but after several hundred yards of ragged prints a fair degree of competence was achieved.

Why were these drawings being produced anyway? The engineering drawing is a communicative document which represents the intention of a creative engineer to produce hardware, his intentions being based upon the specification of the client, in this case the potential ship's owner. The drawing therefore represented hardware some of which would require to be purchased from other firms e.g. main engines, pumps, electric motors, fittings etc and the remainder manufactured e.g. tanks, boilers, pipework, castings for fittings etc. In addition therefore to instructing the shipyard workshops to put the engineroom together in a certain way the drawing on issue was a management instruction to order equipment, stores and plate and also a financial authority to spend a considerable amount of money.

The flow of engineering drawings and prints is therefore an essential part of a thriving engineering industry. The Marine Engineering Department (MED) mainly produced system drawings i.e. scale drawings of the engineroom laid out with the machinery in place. They were often assembly drawings many involving the complex pipework and how it was to run relative to the machinery. But there was original product drawing also in particular tanks, vessels, funnels and boilers. There was also experimental work done, mainly by Mr Wallace the deputy chief draughtsman, and this included e.g. remote valve operation equipment.

In addition to printing drawings a major task of the print boy was to fetch drawings from the safe. The safe was a fireproof , seemingly bombproof, room off the Boilershop entrance hall. This had a massive door and was shelved with hundreds of rolls of drawings going away back probably to the start of the enterprise but certainly including much Foundry engineering works drawings. I know this because on one occasion I had to retrieve a roll dating from the 1920's and the drawing concerned was of an engine built at Lilybank. A ship under repair in Mexico needed a new con rod big end casting and the drawing was located and estimates prepared.

Bill Bruce, one of the respected senior engineering draughtsmen, related to me that on one occasion when facing the prospect of a new design the chief draughtsman Mr McHardy was able to remember a ship having a similar size of intake valve on a ship 30 years previously.

Fetching and returning these rolls was a tedious and dirty job but was punctuated by seeing some interesting drawings including sailing ships.

In parallel with this MED design activity was the main shipbuilding, or hull, design office situated at the shipyard, of which more later. Their work was creating the main structural drawings for the ships and they would supply details of the working spaces for the MED drawing office (DO).

There was also a "Yard Engineering" Department separate from MED which fitted the deck machinery e.g. winches and steering gear on the ships and also maintained the yard steelwork machinery i.e. bending rolls, compressors, riveting guns, shears, cranes etc.

Strangely the MED and the Yard Engineering workers were quite separate entities and generally did not mix.

The print room was gradually getting hotter and this proved to be due to firing up of the large plate furnaces situated close by in the Boilershop. These were large coke fired furnaces which heated the "Scotch boiler" end plates to red heat. These were large semi-circular steel plates about twenty feet or more in diameter and about 1.5 to 2 inches thick and required to have the ends formed over to make a flange all round. When the plate was heated red hot it was pulled out of the furnace on to a large surface-plate where a flange was formed round its edge. A squad of boilermakers clad in damp canvas wraps around their legs and body advanced against this heat for a short session with large hammers to finish the job and pounded the edge of the plate over to finally form a flange all round then they retreated.

This would take some time and several re-heatings before it was finished. This was an impressive process to behold with the men pounding away and the damp canvas smoking from the heat.

The Boilershop held many characters and Wullie told me about an old fitter aged 84 who worked on the repair of pneumatic machinery. This meant he was 28 years of age at the turn of the century.

I visited this old gentleman and it was like meeting someone out of a Dickens story. He was old looking, clad in washed out blue dungarees and greaser, and slightly bent but was otherwise amazing for his age and quite a jolly person. He had a little workshop with windows and his own apprentice and was treated by everyone with great respect.

I now had to learn the delivery part of the job and see much more of the whole enterprise.

The Layout

The delivery of the prints to the various workshops was the next stage and week about would be taken by the print boys in the delivery process. A standard delivery sheet was used with the drawings listed so that each recipient had his consignment of prints entered for that delivery and the foreman signed for the prints. There were two main rounds namely the Boilershop area and the yard area.

The manufacturing units comprised the Boilershop, patternmaker, plumber and machine shop with other addresses including the various fitting out squad foremen on ships building.

On my first delivery I left the office for my Boilershop round laden with a bag full of rolled up drawings and the signing sheet. The first name on the sheet was the Boilermaker foreman (Mr Charles Sturrock).

His office occupied a raised platform 30 feet above the shop floor, shared with a layout floor, in the cavernous Boilershop which had enormous proportions and occupied two bays traversed by 100 ton gantry cranes. The boilermaker craft comprised the measuring, cutting, framing, drilling, joining and assembly of platework into products such as tanks, boilers, pressure vessels, funnels, uptakes and floor-plate systems. There were specialised trades supporting the boilermaker including electric welders, gas burners, blacksmiths and caulkers and there were also semi-skilled machine operators e.g. drill machine operators.

The floor of the Boilershop was earthen and the forming and cutting machines stood gaunt and bleak among piles of plate, angle steel, tanks and vessels and boilers under assembly. Noise permeated the whole building which was essentially corrugated iron on a steel structure, a superb echo chamber, with rooflights of partly blacked out glass, the blackout being a relic of wartime.

The guillotines, plate punches, bending machines, plate rolls and other machine tools had nameplates with the great names of shipbuilding on them, e.g. Hugh Smith, Tangye, and the date of manufacture was not difficult to see on some, the oldest being apparently 1874. These were all black or dull grey adding to the stygian gloom.

The foreman's office or buckie, with windows all round was on a high platform like the bridge of a ship overlooking the Boilershop interior and contained a table and storage for drawings and the foreman's desk. This high platform also appeared to form the "loft" where templates were made to assist in the marking out of plates for cutting and drilling. The "marker-off" also occupied this space he being the senior technical craftsman under the foreman. This man could be the heir apparent as the next foreman, maybe. It would depend whether he had the management skills to take over and sometimes a foreman was brought in from the Tyne or Clyde. The Boilershop drawings were presented and a signature obtained. Another visit in the Boilershop was the workshop of the Boilershop engineer. This was the term used to describe the Boilershop fitting squad foreman. The Boilershop fitters carried out all the engineering fitting work required in connection with tanks, boilers, etc being manufactured in the Boilershop. This work would include the fitting of valves, pipework, sight-glasses. level gauges and other mechanical devices. The fitters workshop was a black dingy greasy smelling "hole in the wall" heated by a Tangye coke stove and was poorly lit, unventilated and had no windows to the outside. While being a grim place it had the singular benefit of being warm and snug, a rare luxury in a shipyard. The fitters likewise were clad in black and dull work clothes and to a man seemed pale and ill. Jock the chargehand signed the sheet and received his blueprints of future work for the squad.

Outside the Boilershop on the west wall was an additional two storey structure called the F.O.S. store (Fitters Out Side). This also housed the headquarters of the marine engineering fitting squads at work on the various ships building or fitting out. (There was some disagreement about whether it meant "fitters outside", "fitters on ship" to mention but two variations but this was resolved for me when I much later met Dr Archibald Hall at University of Dundee who had worked as an apprentice at Lilybank foundry in the 1920's. He said that it meant "fitters outside" to distinguish this lowly breed from the (inside) "cream" engine shop fitters at Lilybank. (These latter were the fitters referred to by Victoria Drummond in her excellent biography by her niece Cherry, the late Baroness Strange)

The Shipyard in which the hulls were built on slipways was distant from the Boilershop and Marine Engineering drawing office by a distance of about one mile to the East and the outside fitting squads could be employed at the Boilershop fitting out jetty the Yard slips or the Yard fitting out jetty where the final stage of fitting out took place. The main reason for the ships to use this Boilershop jetty was to fit all the heavy machinery and boilers making use of the 130 ton cantilever crane, reputedly the heaviest "lift" on the East coast.

The foreman F.O.S., Mr Stevenson, had his office in the F.O.S. store ground floor looking west, the rest of the building being taken up with stores and a light workshop for the jetty. The term FOS had recently been replaced by "Marine Engineering Department" (MED) but old names stuck. A knock on the door, a wait for a response and I went in to obtain the signature of Mr Big. He wore a soft hat, the sure sign of a senior foreman and equal in rank to the bowler. He had several engineroom squad foremen under his command (e.g. Hammy Kinnear, Jim Blyth) attached to ships under construction and in the several years I was to spend in the yard I would seldom see Mr Big outside his "buckie" or office. If a ship were fitting out at the Boilershop there would be a print delivery visit to the engineroom squad foreman for that ship's engineroom but at this time the Boilershop jetty had nothing alongside.

The jetty was solidly built to carry the heavy loads arising from the machinery stored on it. This machinery was the main propulsion engines of a ship in progress on the stocks at the main shipyard and was awaiting assembly in to the engineroom. I took a stroll round to look at the jetty and was immediately impressed by the size of the engine parts stored there. I met the Boilershop rigger,

Wull Gray, who told me the engine was made by the Central Engine works in Hartlepool and was a triple expansion/ exhaust turbine steam engine for the Ellerman ship "Almerian" currently building "on the stocks". I did not know it then but I was looking at the last steam main engine to be fitted into a ship on the Tay and maybe the last in Scotland.

The cold winter wind whipping up the estuary did not encourage me to stay and with my Boilershop round finished I made my way back to the print room for the drawings for the Shipyard delivery.

With my "Yard" consignment of drawings I set out for the Shipyard which was about a one mile walk to the east. As a staff member I did not have to seek a transfer pass from the lodge keeper for the journey as I would have to do later as an apprentice. The walk took me past the LNER main line and one could on occasion see steam locomotives of various types hauling traffic to and from the Aberdeen direction. Also on this walk one passed the works of ICI fittings, and also Hamilton Carharts' workwear factory, the potato depot of Pattullo Barr in the old HMS Ambrose building with rail vans being loaded, J.T.Inglis' proofing works with a pungent ammonia rail tank car outside, the Dundee Power station with its mountain of coal being shaped by a bulldozer and a small Briggs' tar works next to the shipyard.

The shipyard offices were in a substantial important looking building with a lodge. This contained the main commercial offices and the drawing offices of the Naval Architects and this office would on occasion be the first "drop" of the round. In contrast to the casual yet industrious Marine Engineering drawing office at the Boilershop the Yard drawing office (D.O.) was very strictly run by a puritanical chief ship draughtsman Mr Bingham. The draughtsmen were not allowed to smoke and they seemed to be under the thumb of this formal gentleman who reminded me of a rotund but tall Dickensian character.

The assistant chief was a human chap however and signed for the prints allowing me to be on my way and glad to be free of the school-like atmosphere of the place. The way out of the ships' D.O. to the yard was by way of the main building entrance hall in which were on display splendid models of ships recently or notably built by the company and off this gallery through a partly open door could be seen a polished mahogany and leather board room glowing with opulence of yesteryear. The room was lined with trials photographs of past built ships and had a lovely stained glass domed ceiling. This would be the room where launch parties would gather and be entertained prior to proceeding to the launch platform at the ship's bows. A purveyed tea would follow the launch.

I made my way to the double doors exiting the hall and passed through before a clerical looking suited gent. There was an immediate roar of "Come here boy! What's your name, who do you work for? The Engineering Department eh? I might have known!. Astounded, I could only react in shock to this bitter verbal assault from the man who turned out to be the company secretary. This was the sort of gentleman who probably had gone to a "good" school where he learned to treat the working persons with contempt and especially horrid new boys who had not yet learned due deference for this man's importance, or self-importance. It seemed his neurotic response had been based on my neglect to allow this senior person through the door first; after all everybody knew who the company secretary was.

I was to learn that the Shipyard senior management had a lot of types like the "neurotic door man" and I thought that these figures were ill suited to the business of sensitive labour negotiations with labour unions.

The next stop was to the outside marine engineering manager's office where white folded prints, not rolled blue prints, had to be filed in the manager's plan boxes. The building, mentioned earlier at my interview, was a flat roofed two storey weatherboard structure with a central corridor and offices off on both sides. The corridor was interesting in that the various offices had notices over the doors of the resident officers of the shipping companies which had tonnage under construction at the yard. These included Ellerman Lines, Alfred Holt, Blue Star line, Lloyds Inspectors etc.

These offices were all at the main gate area of the yard and the next task was to find the patternmakers workshop located in the main joiner's shop. The patternmakers produced wooden models or moulding patterns of fittings such as valves, hand-wheels, brackets etc. These patterns were then sent to an outside foundry for the production of castings which would be returned to the Yard, machined and assembled into machinery for the ships concerned. The Caledon used among others a foundry located at Denny in Stirlingshire and also for non-ferrous castings Boswells of Dock Street Dundee.

The pattern maker chargehand signed the sheet for the blueprints and guidance was sought for the next stop namely "C/hand fitter 702". This was the address of the chargehand fitter on a ship No 502 "Almerian" engine No 702, building on the stocks at slip No1. The way to the chargehand's buckie involved passing plating and frame shops which were large gloomy partly open sided

68

corrugated iron structures dimly lit by feeble lamps such that marking out was done at wall-less places where natural light could get in. Here too were the great smoking coal fired frame furnaces which heated the ships' skeletal frames to red heat so that they could readily be formed into curves by a group of burlap clad hammermen. These furnaces produced an ever present smoky haze in the frame shop and laid down a layer of ash everywhere. This was however a popular place for workers to collect at starting time on a cold and frosty morning, chew the fat, and choose the days horses from the Daily Record.

Being now in the heart of the yard the impression was one of noise, smoke, human effort and iron oxide and the ever present moan or whine of cranes working. These cranes were lifting on board the ship pumps, fittings, ducts, plates, skips, pipes and the multitude of other items required in the building activity.

Walking down the side of an embrionic ship on Slip No1 I located the chargehand fitter of "702" namely Shug Hart. The buckie (or hut) was a wooden shed holding the drawings and other engineering paperwork for the ship's engineroom. The small shed had some form of electric heating and this provided such buckies with a characteristic smell like hot tallow which approximates to the smell of rancid bacon fat. I introduced myself to the chargehand fitter who signed the delivery sheet and put the roll of blueprints on the congested shelf above his bench. The seeming confusion of drawings did not appear to represent the order which must emerge in a modern engine room but as I was to find later the practice of engineering would often mean retaining masses of information to eventually provide the finished product this being a good example of the tremendous information patterning capacity of the human brain.

It was something of a disappointment to me to find that the appearance of these "Engineers" as they were called was not anything special at all, indeed they looked like ordinary workmen such as plumbers or joiners. I had expected the engineer to be a leading employee clad in at least a white coat and involved in a clean precision like environment. The truth was beginning to dawn that things were not going to be as I had imagined. In fact the men I was seeing were engineering fitters, some of them very good craftsmen, but I was to find out later that the term "Engineer" was a most abused title.

The next stage of the walk passed the top of the slips and a ship, seen to be nearing launch, was the "MV Diomed" for the high quality Blue Funnel shipping line of Alfred Holt Ltd of Liverpool (or its subsidiaries such as Ocean Shipping).

Deeper into the yard to the East the next stop was the Marine Engineering Dept. machine shop known as "D" shed which like all workshop buildings in the shipyard was steel framed with corrugated iron cladding. This was the darkest, gloomiest machine shop I had ever seen, partly due to the fact that the windows still had on their wartime blackout and partly because the matt black lathes, drills borers and earthen floors absorbed the light. Several yellowing light bulbs struggled to radiate light. The workmen also wore matt black and blended into the general murk of the place. It was the sort of workshop that looked the same whether on day or night shift. On the earthen floor near to their mother machines were stacked newly machined gleaming parts of steel, cast iron or brass. Heating was by a coke fired Tangye stove.

I picked my way to the foreman's buckie. He was David Forbes a spry short round man in a dark blue pinstripe suit, including waistcoat and Albert, and a cloth cap which was tweed coloured, multi piece, in contrast to the greasy one piece caps of the machine craftsmen. I thus collected another signature and was told that in the near future I should deliver the drawings to the new "D" shed next door.

It was strange that any human being could become attached to working in such grimy conditions but as I was to learn men would fight tooth and nail for their right to do so. The conditions I was seeing were common in engineering workshops all over the UK and had probably looked much the same in Victorian times.

However from the foreman's instructions it appeared the building of a new workshop was nearing completion and I looked forward to seeing it.

The Coppersmiths shop was next with plans for the foreman. This was where the copper pipes, large and small, for the engineroom were produced. It was impressive to see the large e.g. 14 inch diameter pipes being filled with sand or pitch and bent into complex shapes.

The Plumbers shop was also visited as this shop produced the steel pipes for the ship including engineroom pipes.

The final stop on the tour was delivery of the few prints for the MED foreman's buckie on the Yard fitting out jetty otherwise known as the Caledon East fitting out jetty. Fewer fitters were necessary at this stage of construction as work was nearing completion and engineroom commissioning and "stand-by" were well under way. The ship alongside was "City of Winnipeg" a motor ship circa 8,500 tons gross for the City shipping line. This looked to be a much more acceptable situation as here was a real ship with gleaming paintwork, funnel, windows, lit up portholes and even engines running down below.

Print boys were not permitted on board the vessels building and we were given severe warnings about this. The prohibition reflected the real dangers in shipyard work and the insurance cover relating to types of staff.

One annoying feature however was the preponderance of hoses and cables joining ship to shore which gave the impression of chaos. These lines were air for power tools such as drills, caulking and riveting and hand held grindstones. There was also electric power for welders and temporary lights.. The ship was by now generating much of its power required for lighting and driving pumps and other auxiliaries.

Such was the first day's delivery and I returned to the print room at the distant Boilershop.

The Detail

The period in the printroom of the MED drawing office was to be the prelude to the start of my apprenticeship at the age of 16, this becoming due in August 1956. The drawing office premises were post 1st World War vintage but had about them the air of Victoriana prevalent in engineering works everywhere. A spur railway track led into the Boilershop alongside the drawing offices and on occasion a diesel locomotive would shunt plate wagons into the Boilershop passing below the Drawing office windows. On occasion a steam engine would be used, usually a 4 wheel "Pug", probably ex-Caledonian, with a spark arrestor on its chimney. This produced a roar and flurry of steam and lovely smelling coal smoke.

The draughtsmen worked at long horizontal drawing boards 42 inches wide and up to 12 feet long.

On these boards great sheets of strong tracing paper were drawn upon by the draughtsmen. These drawings were of machinery arrangements, piping drawings for e.g. oil fuel, lubrication oil and domestic water. There were also schematic drawings, and drawings of specific parts such as boilers, tanks and valves.

These drawings would occupy a board for months and would become dry and brittle rendering them liable to damage in the printing process. When the drawings were finished and after first-off prints had been made they were traced in ink onto blue glossy linen by female tracers who were the female glamour in DO's up and down the country.

The chief draughtsman occupied a glazed office giving a wide view of his domain in two directions though he never seemed to use this visual facility but was perpetually engrossed in paperwork on his desk peering through the smoke from his lip grasped cigarette.

No office would be complete without the office girls who provided typing services, operated the telephone exchange and supplied the office tea.

In this system I performed the function of print boy and among the first difficulties was getting in tune with the daily system or routine. The days were long and not terribly exciting since the print boy was not involved in the engineering business that went on there. However there were moments such as the "oiling incident". My fellow print boy Jim and I had been in the job about ten days when, during a brief spell of Wullie's absence, Jim decided that it might be a good idea to do something useful.

White prints were developed in an "Ozalid" continuous rolling type of machine which exposed the photo-sensitive paper to ammonia fumes and produced the blue dyeline copy of the original drawing. An electric motor drove the machine via a small worm and wheel gearbox the size of a tea caddy. If one unscrewed a stopper in the roof of this gearbox the gears could be seen churning away in their amply greased environment. Jim took the oil can and presented it to the gearbox but instead of dropping oil through the hole he inserted it into the box whereupon the gears got hold of it in an "Ingoing nip" and crunched the end off the oil can. But worse still this event had stripped the teeth off one of the gears and the print machine ceased to run, the transmission being broken. The oil can was thrown to the far end of a dull cupboard in the printroom and a pretence of normality was assumed.

On Wullie's return the first time the ammonia machine was required it was found mysteriously not to be taking in paper for developing. Wullie soon twigged that the gearbox was out of action. "What have you guys been up to?" he asked, silence was his reply.

The Ozalid man was called and soon had the machine working again and he wondered why the failure should have occurred. Wullie got it out of us however on an occasion when he was recommending frankness in all things. The cat was out of the bag but to his credit he did not act rashly by attempting punishment rather he wisely used the incident to illustrate that honesty really was the best policy and that "Laddies shouldnae try tae be engineers before their time."

Wullie's main extra-mural, or even mural, activity was running the Macrae Boy's Club in Glenagnes Road in the city and many of the messages I ran uptown were connected with the club. This could include a bike trip up to Watts in the Wellgate with a message re a weekend concert to a pianist called Cathie McCabe or along to the brickworks of Dunbrik at Stannergate to arrange a price with Mr Gouick for off-standard bricks for a wall at the club. One design task I was given was a plan for a design for a greenhouse complex and garden for the club.

I had never drawn such a thing before but nevertheless gave it a try based on my technical drawing experience at school. The result seemingly impressed as it was done in isometric view i.e. a view which gives a three-dimensional effect.

This drawing was to assist me later in gaining entry to the drawing office during my engineering apprenticeship when Wullie would retrieve it from one of his strangely oil stained cupboards on an enquiry from the chief draughtsman about "this laddie they are sending up for interview".

Other "messages" included trips to firms such as Payne's plating shop at West Port, Blackness foundry, Thows the engravers in Wellgate for an engine nameplate, McCara's the sheet metal workers in Dock St or Boswells the brass foundry also in Dock St. The purpose would be an emergency drawing delivery or to pick up a small item needed in a rush.

It is surprising to note that during this time as a print boy there was still no clear concept of what was involved in the task of being an "Apprentice engineer". It would dawn on me slowly that dirty blue boilersuits would be the mode of dress rather than spotless white and the mode of work would be more metalwork in nature rather than technical work on engine systems. Of course the proper term should have been "Apprentice fitter" a noble and undervalued craft training.

But there seemed to be a considerable time to get through before the start of apprenticeship, eight months, and at that time it seemed an age and correspondingly boredom set in. Once the skills of wielding the trimming razor had been mastered and blueprinting and white printing executed several dozen times it seemed anything would be better than working in the dismal print room.

It is worth noting the venerable characters in the MED drawing office at that time especially the bowler hatted brothers Adamson. Sandy was chief engineering estimator and Harry was a draughtsman. Mr (Sandy) Adamson, trim moustachioed suited, passed through the print-room every day on his way to the estimator's office. Estimators were experienced engineering draughtsmen who specialised in costing enquiries for new ship's enginerooms. These brothers were over 70 at the time and still working full time. They had probably both worked at Lilybank foundry which had closed in the early 1930's.

Sandy Adamson related to me once how in his young days at Lilybank the prints were made in glass frames on the roof of the drawing office with solar exposure as the light source.

The Adamson brothers were said not to speak to each other at all. They were old gentlemen at that time and would not be there three years later when I returned to take a board in the drawing office as an apprentice engineering draughtsman. It was related to me that when Sandy eventually retired it was found that he had been using a valuable data book of his own notes which assisted him in his work. It is said that it took the charm of Yard estimating Director Mr John Liddle to get Sandy to surrender the book as Caledon property.

Mr Stewart, the engineering manager hailing from Scotts of Greenock, was another who had high office in the MED. He was the senior resident engineering manager at the Boilershop and was approaching retirement at the time I was in the print room. While I was there he designed "Scotch" boilers which was one of the higher technical tasks undertaken in MED. Not surprisingly boilers were one of the most technically demanding products made at the boiler shop and Mr Stewart appeared to keep this job to himself. An engineering director, Mr W.O. Gardner, had recently been appointed and the engineering manager position would fade out when Mr Stewart retired.

William McHardy was the chief draughtsman with Bert Wallace his deputy. Other Senior draughtsmen at the time included Mr Kelso, Tom Elder, Bill Bruce, John Taylor, David Harley, Sid Sime, Jim Prophet, John McSheffrey and estimators Mr Boyd and Charlie Donaldson.

As my 16th birthday approached I had had enough of being a print boy and I looked forward to starting my apprenticeship.

Starting my time

And so after the annual holiday break during which the entire industry of the town shut down it was time to report to the Engineering foreman of the Marine Engineering Department (MED).

The meeting was at 7.30am this being an early hour compared to the 8.45 start of the print room days. I had been issued with two brass checks, rectangular brass coin like things the size of a large postage stamp with the number 2279 stamped upon them. One of these was to be handed in at the end of each half day and picked up at the timekeepers "boley" at the start of each half day. If one minute or more past the starting time 15 minutes were removed from one's pay hence the term "quartered". Between 15 minutes and 30 minutes the penalty was 30 minutes lost and a chit from the foreman was required in order to get the check from the timekeeper. The handing in process on leaving e.g. at lunchtime was a misnomer because the workmen waited as a crowd inside the gates just before finishing time and surged forward en masse like a football crowd when the gates opened. Finishing times were 12 noon and 5.18 pm. This gave a 44 hour week. The checks then literally rained into a large box fixed to the gate.

These checks were then collected, many from the ground, by the timekeeper who was of the same ilk as that sort of person who becomes a gillie or gamekeeper.

On the morning of starting my apprenticeship and at Mr Stevenson's door waiting his convenience I wished that I had access to such a thing as a "used boilersuit" shop so that the new apprentice did not look quite so new and "green" in his dark blue spotless overall. This foreman was in charge of the entire labour force of MED engineering tradesmen and would have little direct contact with me other than to allocate me to No 708 ship's engine room squad on the ship building on the stocks at the yard. This meeting with the foreman was at the Boilershop and was in his office in the FOS store.

Thus allocated to a ship, or "boat" more commonly, the first duty was to draw tools these being two heavy spanners, 5/8" and ¾"Whitworth , and a 1-1/4 lb hammer. I started the same morning as Doug Westwood whose pre-apprenticeship job had been as a store-boy in the FOS store and who knew the ropes regarding drawing tools. We then set off for the yard some 20 mins distant having picked up a transfer pass from the Boilershop lodge. This recorded the time on leaving the Boilershop and was handed in on arriving at the yard. This practice marked the boundary over which I had passed from the white collar job to the blue collar. The first being trusted the second not.

We arrived at the yard surrendered the pass and sought the then chargehand on "708" (later named "Canadian Star") Wullie Christie. This led to more waiting around until he arrived from the ship and he then thought about what he was to do with these new "laddies". Apprentices were rarely referred to as such, more as laddies than anything else. Jobs in hand for the MED people when the ship was fitting out on the stocks (or slips as they became at a later stage) were the installation of below waterline valves, i.e. sea valves, tail shaft and propeller plus other equipment such as generators, pumps, piping and light machinery. Sea valves were fitted to studs set in "welded on" pads inside the hull . The pad, welded to the ship's side, had to have the joint face filed flat to mate with the valve so that a long lasting water tight seal could be made. Clearly if these valves failed a very serious situation could develop in the engineroom with the sea leaking in to the bilges.

We were sent to work with two fitters working on these valves namely one Hamish Watson a recently time served journeyman returned from national service and an older ex-Calcutta mills fitter who had recently come to work in the yard.

One learned not to ask too many questions about ones workmates so I never did find out much about the journeymen I worked for other than that volunteered from time to time.

The ship at this stage was a bare rusty steel environment with staging, i.e. planks on supports, all round the ship's side inside and out. This was a depressive environment but an engineroom had to start somewhere and go through this basic stage. I was warned to watch out for the stagers who arranged the working platforms and could drop things.

In fitting the sea valves, which the journeymen were allocated, there was no air of urgency and the job was approached tangentially via much talking and irrelevancies.

The journeymen did the filing and fitting and the apprentices were sent for parts from the stores. On sea valves the brass studs were screwed through the pad on the ship's side from the outside using a square on the head of the stud. The valve, with a joint, was then mounted on the studs and nuts tightened up over the washer and "grommets". Grommets, said to be made by prisoners, were string woven into a ring like a small lifebelt and soaked in a red lead and raw linseed oil mixture, this forming a seal under the nut and washer. Red lead was used widely in the yard mainly as the first coat of paint on the bare steel. I knew it to be poisonous and took great care with it. The squared head on the stud was then sawn off and filed smooth.

The shipyard day was 7.30 to 12.00 and 1.00 to 5.18 punctuated by breaks at 9am and 3pm. These breaks were unofficial and both sides played out a charade regarding them. The fact was that work stopped for about 20 mins and prior to this the apprentices were sent off to make the tea in an old syrup tin (can) with a wire handle. The task was to find a riveting squad and place the can on the coke fire used to heat rivets. It was accepted by the men that this would happen and there could be several cans heating at once and the heater boy could at the same time be dispensing red-hot rivets to his squad. Heater boys were not usually boys but could be quite mature or even elderly men.

The tea cans were then carried back carefully to the engine room. The men then stood round in groups having their tea break with piece (sandwich) and pursuing several lines of wayside philosophy.

The working environment was noisy, gloomy and dangerous. Two trades, the riveters and the caulkers, were responsible for most of the noise. In 1956 the ships still had numerous riveted sections where the ship designers had not yet given in to welding.

Riveting was a method of joining drilled plates by overlapping them then inserting a red hot headed rivet into the hole and its end hammered over. On cooling, and contracting, the rivet held the plates very tightly indeed creating a watertight joint..

The man inserting the rivet and holding it there was called a holder-on and the man hammering it on the other side of the plate was the riveter. The rivets were heated by a heater boy and the hot rivets were conveyed to the holder on by a catch-boy. The four made up a typical riveting squad.

Red hot rivets could commonly be seen flying through the air on their way to the holder-on and on one occasion a large glowing rivet landed some yards in front of me when walking alongside a ship on the stocks.

This process had been developed from that used in boiler making when iron was first used in the construction of ships. Hence the reason that steel workers in the yards were members of the Boilermakers union. Incidentally in shipyards the steel trades who heated formed or joined steel were collectively known as the "black squad" and comprised e.g. riveters, holders on, caulkers, platers, burners and welders. They were usually on a form of piece work while other trades such as engineering fitters, joiners, plumbers, coppersmiths, carpenters, riggers, holeborers, painters and shipwrights were time trades.

Time trades were in fact paid a kind of bonus called "Paid by Results" (PBR) but their pay was inferior to that of the black squad.

I was able to observe various trades at work round the engineroom and the impression I got was that the black squad trades got on with the job and spent little time talking or hanging about. This was perhaps to be expected since their pay was tied to their measured output. However it was said that restrictive practices were in force which limited productivity.

The management of time trades at this stage of construction was poor as though there was not enough work to go round and it had to be eked out. This poor management plus poor wages coupled to low output was, I believe, a core contributor to the demise of shipyards.

After work on the fitting of sea valves the next job was filing the flanges of a mountain of pipes which had been lifted by crane into the hold forward of the engineroom. This boded ill and much boring work lay ahead. Somehow it did not happen that way. I started at Dundee Technical College (now Abertay University) for one day per week and this upset one's allocation to a journeyman (the term for a time served tradesman).

The ship construction was proceeding and the hole in the ship's side affording entry to the engineroom was closed up in preparation for making the hull watertight. This meant that everyone going on board had to ascend a gangway up the ships side and then descend a very long ladder down into the engine room. On one occasion when returning to the ship from an errand rather than go up the gangway I ascended one of the vertical staging stanchions along the side of the ship. I went up about 70 feet hand over hand then walked the 6-foot long 2 inch wide beam to the deck. I shudder to think of it in retrospect.

I assisted with fitting pipes to pumps, valves to tanks and similar jobs. I was able to visit a ship in the last stages of completion at the East fitting out berth. The process was that a ship was launched and towed to the Boilershop fitting out jetty where the 130 ton crane was situated. After some months there and with the heavy equipment and funnel fitted the ship was moved to the East fitting out jetty at the shipyard.

A ship I visited at the latter jetty was the Ellerman lines' "Almerian" which was undergoing dock trials of the main engines. This was the first trial of the main engines now coupled up to the propeller and the ship was especially firmly held by hawsers to the jetty and the engines started. This was always great moment in a ships life and was something I wanted to see.

A ship on dock trials is becoming alive and the smells were characteristic of a hot working engineroom in contrast to the arid cold engine space of a ship on the stocks. I entered the engineroom, with its hot oil smell, from above looking down through a forest of gratings to the three engine cylinder heads. Down deeper into the engineroom I encountered the gleaming rotating main engine crankshaft and a groaning Weir's air pump which evacuated the condenser. Through a doorway in the bulkhead I visited the stokehold, where the boilers are situated, and saw the three great oil fired "Scotch" boilers, which I had seen being made at the Boilershop during my print room era. These oil fired boilers with their deep throated furnace roar were producing superheated steam at 300 pounds per square inch for the triple expansion engine with exhaust turbine which I had seen at the Boilershop "in waiting" earlier that year. It was a magnificent sight to see the Central Engineworks' Marine triple expansion engine running with synchronised ease. This type of engine was open-crankcase and one could see the motion of the gleaming connecting rods and crankshaft creating the power for the propeller shaft. An Auerbach exhaust turbine was also fitted adding to the engine output.

I had a feeling that this was the last steam main engined ship to be built on the Tay and this has proven to be so. Coincidentally steam engine building was also finishing on the railways as the "Evening Star" the last steam locomotive to be built in Britain was building at BR engineering works Swindon about this time.

Transfer to D Shed

My time on the stocks with 708 was soon to be limited by my transfer to the new "D" shed which was the MED machine shop. The job here was to work with my new journeyman fitter Bert Mathers who assembled valves for use in ship's engine rooms. There were about five such fitters and the valve types included angle and globe types and cocks in materials such as cast iron, bronze and cast steel. These would be used in the ships for controlling fluid flow the common fluids being fresh and sea water, oil, steam, air and also cargo fluids such as palm oil or molasses. Bert's previous apprentice had been called "the barber" and had made extra money at lunchtime giving haircuts.

The Caledon unusually retained the manufacture of its own valves which could probably be purchased cheaper from a high volume manufacturer. "D shed" was probably the last remaining part of the Lilybank engineering works which had had the ability to produce everything from nuts and bolts, valves, pumps, boilers and marine engines. The new D shed was light and airy and oil fired warm air heating was fitted. Bert was about 57 and had been an orphan before serving his time in Wallace Foundry in Brown Constable Street prior to world War1. He had volunteered and served with the RN on a monitor in WW1.

Bert had high standards but like many shipyard fitters he had learned to pace the work. It is easy to criticize this attitude but many of these chaps had experienced the 30's Depression and did not wish to work themselves out of a job. A typical valve (see sketch below) comprises a body, flanges, a seat, a valve plug, a spindle a bridge a gland, pillars and handwheel. The parts were machined in D shed from castings and stock bar and assembled by the fitters into the finished valve. Bert insisted on finishing the

86

bridge by draw filing and virtually polishing it which seemed to me a waste of effort. However he did give me much guidance and I learned from him.

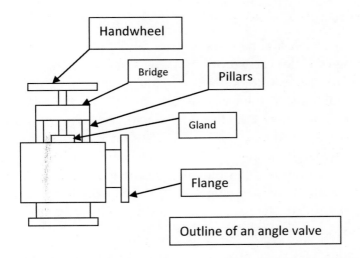

Handwheel

Bridge

Pillars

Gland

Flange

Outline of an angle valve

Bert had worked in the Caledon in the twenties on fitting sea valves. He spoke of a ship called the "Atlantian". At that time before the advent of "welded on" pads inside the hull sea valves had to be fitted to the curve of the ships side which meant much hard and precise filing work before bolting them on. These had been tough times and typical of shipyard work where the job could finish at any time and usually did when the ship was completed. He had served his apprenticeship at the Wallace foundry and worked in other foundries in Dundee including a firm which serviced stationary gas engines. This included one job at Westhall quarry Murroes at which the boss could usefully be seen in the distance approaching in his car He also described working at Halleys engineering works in Lindsay Street where textile machinery was made (now Dundee Council Main Office).

They also manufactured hackles, i.e. a segmental drum with thousands of sharp pins fitted and used for carding textile prior to spinning. These pins were also made there on a grinding machine forming the sharp points. He had also worked on French circular looms at Wallace foundry in Dundee in the early 1950's.

So "D" shed was a new experience and gave an insight to machining of metal carried out by turners and machinemen , not fitters. Most of the work was valve manufacture from 2-inch bore up to about 14 inch bore and associated fittings e.g. tee-pieces, bends etc but there was the occasional variation for outside customers instanced by dressing cylinders for Blackness foundry. These were large drums 5 feet diameter by 6 feet long with spindles, or trunnions, on the ends and they were used in jute fibre preparation for spinning. The assembly of these involved riveting the rolled plate surface to the end plates and fitting the trunnions.

This riveting was done outside D shed but they were brought in for machining the trunnions true and skimming the drum surface smooth. This employed the largest lathe in D Shed having a great 20ft long bed and 6ft diameter faceplate. It is likely that this had been a crankshaft lathe from elsewhere in Dundee, most likely Lilybank Foundry.

I worked on lifting gear for the ships engineroom and also safety rails for several of the machines in D shed. My most creative moment however was my design and manufacture of a tap lever for my toolbox. Apprentices usually made some of their own tools and tap levers were a common example.

A tap is a hard cutting screw used for cutting screw threads in holes. This has to be rotated by hand by means of the square on its end. A tap lever is used for this task and therefore needs a square hole to fit the tap. My special problem was that I had quite a small toolbox being a wooden ammunition box converted for the purpose. The normal design of lever would not fit in the box so I designed a dismantle-able lever. It was about 16 inches overall length.

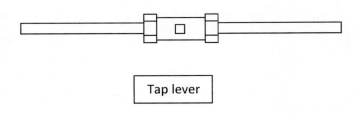

Tap lever

This design allowed one arm to be disconnected and it fitted in the box quite well then.

This, surprisingly, was a revolutionary design and was copied by others during my time "on the tools". An example of this was when an apprentice, Frank McPhilips, was sent to find me on board a ship in order to borrow the lever to copy it. Incidentally Frank was much later covered in black fuel oil when a loading pipe burst in the engine-room of a ship fitting out. He was hustled away to the ambulance room to be cleaned up and was none the worse for the experience. The last I heard of him was that he was working in Hollywood California. It was also borrowed by the foreman to lend to the repair squad which was working on a coaster in the dry dock. They had to tap a hole on the sterntube system but there was no room to rotate a normal tap lever, but if one arm could be removed as in my tap lever the job could be done. But, back to the ships.

Engineering my future

To the Ships Again

While the D shed work was warm and indoors it was a factory type environment and I was keen to pass on to something else when the opportunity arose after 8 months.

A young person prefers the free-er atmosphere of fitting out on the ships. I was transferred to a Holt ship fitting out on the stocks namely Engine No 710 "Menelaus" and was placed with a journeyman named Jim Durie nicknamed "Durex Jim". This nickname arose because Jim would buy contraceptives for some of the older apprentices who were too shy to buy them themselves. Jim was a good man and was a model journeyman to have. He did not use foul language gratuitously as did many. The job he was allocated was mainly pipe fitting that is assembling and jointing the engineroom pipes and fittings making up the various fluid systems e.g. fuel, cooling water and lubricating oil.

I was not with Jim long as he already had another apprentice and I was transferred to work with "Jock the Rat". He was man about 45-50, lean in body and head and about 5'11" with hair greased down making him rodent like. He wore the greasiest boilersuit imaginable which I never saw clean. He was not particularly well liked by many because of his abnoxious ways but that did not bother him.

His specialist job was keepers. These are the clamps, of which there are many hundreds, which hold engineroom pipes securely connected to the structure. It was the practice that certain fitters would do the same job ship after ship such as main engine, generators, marking out etc and, in this case, keepers.

The keeper job was not terribly complex. The keepers were made to order from the Boilershop blacksmiths. The fitter's job was to measure up and order the keepers, select the position of the keeper

91

on the pipe and arrange for a bar to be cut to size and welded to place on a structural member. The apprentice did much of the bar measuring and running to a tradesman burner (oxy acetylene cutter) to get it cut to size. This was then returned to the journeyman fitter who held it in place for the welder to fix. This connection has to be to an appropriate place e.g. not to the ships shell plates nor to a tank above the oil level in a tank but mainly to a frame or substructure. All of this took place in an engine room full of noise dust and gloom. The main engine was in place by this time and the engine room was a beehive of noisy activity with temporary hoses temporary lights and cables everywhere serving the myriad trades involved. These trades included plumbers, electricians, laggers (using asbestos), welders, coppersmiths, boilermakers, riveters, burners, caulkers, painters, sheetmetal workers etc.

The Rat was not someone the apprentice got to know, he was a cold, ill-tempered person given to drink in his own time but having a hangover on many occasions. The apprentice to him was a gopher, not much else. Of course the apprentice was also expected to make the tea in the communal can but with such as the Rat I chose to get my own can. Apprentices were sent off to find a riveter's fire over which the tea-can was suspended. One story of tea-making involved "The barber" an apprentice fitter who was a keen hill walker. He was returning from heating two cans, one in each hand, and his chosen path was via a narrow 3 inch wide grating bracket, between the main engine and one of the engine room flats i.e. the galleries which form the side areas of the engine room. The barber slipped and fell but managed to keep his legs round the bracket and was suspended upside down 30 feet above the engineroom floor. An agile young man he avoided injury but most importantly , it is said, there was not a drop of the tea spilled.

92

The time with the Rat was interrupted by my taking the Asian Flu and I was off work for three weeks.

On returning to the ship I was allocated to another journeyman namely Jim Whitton who was the "watertight door man". To explain, the wall which forms the stern side of the engineroom is called the aft bulkhead. The shafting tunnel leads from this bulkhead at tank-top level and contains the propeller shaft. The doorway to this tunnel must in emergency be closed by a watertight door which isolates the engineroom from the propeller shafting tunnel. The rods to operate the door led up to an upper deck to allow remote closing. Jim's task was to fit the rods (or operating shafts) and mechanisms to operate the door.

Jim had been at the shipyard for a number of years formerly being a textile works mechanic with no marine experience prior to his time at the Caledon. He was a pleasant if a bit enigmatic person compared to the Rat. He did not like to have many questions.

The apprentice's job here was to assist in lining up the bearing systems for the shafts and preparing the stools, or supports, for the bearings. The shafts were measured up drilled and pinned to their couplings and assembled to place. There was however much standing about and I would have preferred a busier and progressive involvement. Jim was not any worse in this respect than any other journeyman but there was in the shipyard time trades a culture of "spinning things out" or "this is a good job, if it gets finished early the next one may be awful". As noted previously there were two major groups of manual workers i.e. the bonus or piece work trades i.e. those who were paid on what they produced, and the time trades.

The black squad was paid mainly by piece work while the engineering and others e.g. joiners, plumbers etc were paid a

93

weekly wage with a little PBR as mentioned earlier. In Engineering this led to a feeling of resentment and may have led to the unhurried culture. It was said that a plater's helper, an unskilled steelwork labourer, on a good week earned more than an engineering fitter. This was a management fault which was, in my view, not conducive to good productivity.

About this time the ship was moved from the Boilershop down to the fitting out quay at the shipyard. The watertight door job was ultimately finished and Jim was allocated his other job of fitting nameplates to valves. This was a reasonably good job and gave one the opportunity to learn something of the systems in the engineroom. Each valve had a cast brass name plate fitted to it showing its function. Jim would read the drawing (at threepence an hour extra) and tie the nameplate to the valve. My job was to follow up and drill the valve body to take two "hammer in" pins which held the plate in place and then fit the plate.

The engineroom was now in an advanced state, the main engines had been fitted and the Allen V8 diesel generators were working full time. It was not a bad place to be when the weather was still cold.

The starting of the diesel main engines for the first time was an exciting event as many things would be put to the test. Menelaus was for the Blue Funnel line (Alfred Holt Ltd) and had a 6 cylinder Burmeister and Wain opposed piston main engine. This was an enormous engine having cylinders of 750 mm diameter and stood about 30 feet high above the tank top and was approximately 50 feet long. It was started by introducing compressed air into the cylinders which gave the engine enough motion to fire.

It was a magnificent sight to see such a massive machine run. It was an opposed piston crosshead engine which means it had these crosshead beams above the cylinders rising and falling at engine speed. It ran at about 100 revs/min and was surprisingly quiet save for the regular dull ping of the diesel firing in the cylinders.

Work on the ship was running out and we were transferred to the Boilershop jetty to one of a pair of ships being built for the Bowater line, the "Elizabeth Bowater". These were pulp carriers for the Bowater paper company and each was to be fitted with a Clark North Eastern Marine-Sulzer main engine i.e. a Sulzer design made under licence by Clark NE Marine on the Tyne. It was for me a let-down to go back to the cold rusty basic engineroom stage but that was the kind of business it was.

The watertight door gear was not ready to fit and we were then allocated to main engine work which may seem like a good job but involved a lot of heavy slogging work on engine assembly. This included tightening "slogging up" the main cylinder bolts and the largely dreaded chock fitting.

Chocks are cast iron blocks upon which the main engine sits supported by the tank top. I should explain that the "tank top" is the floor of the engineroom which is formed by the top plates of the double bottom tanks and which carries the main engine on thick plates known as the engine sheet.

When the main engine is lined up using temporary wedges to the propeller shaft there is a space between the engine bedplate bottom and the tank top engine plate. Into this space many chocks are fitted in line with the holding down bolts. These chocks were solid cast iron blocks about 280mm by 300mm by 55mmthick.

The fitters job was to fit the chock by grinding and filing so that a 1.5 thousandth of an inch feeler could not enter anywhere round the edge. The chock was then drilled through to take a "fitted" holding down bolt. "Fitted" here means the bolt was a neat fit in the hole which was drilled and reamed by a tradesman called a "hole borer". The bolt, smeared with white lead, was passed up from the double bottom tank area and the nut screwed on thus securing the engine bedplate to the tank top.

Chock fitting was a hated job by some fitters. It was a test of skill and largely in public. It was also exposed to rain and snow. While working on this job I was sent for and told to report to a ship on the stocks namely Ellerman Line "City of Hereford" and to join the "tunnel squad".

Engineering my future
Tunnel and Main Engine

On the appointed day I carried my toolbox to the ship on the stocks which at that stage was a rusty hull with no engine, shaft or propeller. I made my way to the stern where a scaffolding had been erected round the sternpost area to allow access for the tunnel squad. I was spotted by one of the squad who told me to bring my box up to the staging.

The tunnel squad's job was to bore out the sternpost, which is a large steel casting to carry the rudder, to take the sterntube in which rotates the tailshaft section which in turn carries the propeller. The other lengths of shafting are added inboard in the shafting tunnel and bearings fitted. The main engine is then connected to the shafting. The sterntube, tailshaft and propeller have to be fitted before launch of the ship so the tunnel squad are one of the earliest of the engineering squads on the ship. The shaft would typically be about 15 to18 inches diameter and the propeller about 14 feet diameter or more so this was quite heavy engineering.

The squad comprised four fitters, four helpers, a chargehand (Shug Rogers) and an apprentice.

This squad operated independently of the engineroom squad and had their own store area in a corner of the yard and a handbarrow. Not many squads could boast a handbarrow.

The first stage of boring out is to set up a straight line of steel wire, representing the shafting centreline from engineroom to sternpost so that the bore will be in line (lining out). This distance could be up to 200 feet. Propulsion shafting has to be straight and precise in a hull which is not. Lining out was carried out after working hours in a quiet hull and usually meant all-night working

97

by the squad. Extra pay at time and half was payable with double time next day if worked.

The work was critical and was under the supervision of the marine engineering manager, at the time in question Mr J. Anderson.

When the wire was taught corrective supports were placed to take out much of the catenary sag in wire. Using the wire as the centre line the fitters marked out by centre punch the aft peak bulkheads and sternpost to take the sterntube.

This was my first "all nighter" and I was now allowed to work overtime having become eighteen earlier that year. It was a strange experience working in a quiet hull and also a risky job one having to squat in the aft peak from bulkhead edge to bulkhead edge above a dark chasm down to the aft peak bilges. However it did not take all night and when the marking out was complete at about 2am some shuteye was achieved before 6.30 am when we could go home for breakfast.

We returned at 7.30 to put in a full day but admittedly a tiring one.

With the line out established and marked a boring out rig was assembled on the sternpost. This comprised a solid 6 inch diameter shaft with a cutting tool holder which rotated and machined a circular hole in the steel sternpost and bulkheads to the fitters'marks. The boring out process could take several weeks and had to proceed in all weather sometimes with the waves breaking below..

The boring rig was of course perched above the river which at high tide would be below us. In winter this was a most inhospitable place especially if one was suffering from a cold. Canvas wind sheets were erected but the draughts were unbeatable.

The tunnel squad had a certain prestige and reputation to uphold. It had a toughness and independence associated with it based upon its clear role, the need to contend with the elements and the only engineering squad with the authority to machine the hull structure.

When the boring out was complete the sterntube was shipped inboard and fitted nicely the hole we had bored for it. This involved much careful work with lifting tackle and could be dangerous work. The great tube weighing several tons was inched into place from the shaft tunnel side and when in position bolted fast to the bulkhead. New cranes had recently been installed alongside the slipways of 15tons capacity.

The next principal component was the tailshaft i.e the part of the propeller shaft which is connected to the propeller. This runs in the sterntube which, with the ship later in the water, is awash with seawater as a lubricant but has a gland at the aft bulkhead to keep out the sea from the tunnel. Fitting this heavy shaft, of approximately 5 tons weight, was also a careful inching process and I was instructed to get between the ship's frames and stay there in case a sling broke or a tackle failed.

The tailshaft end now stuck out of the end of the ship waiting the propeller. For this job another trade, the rigger, was brought in to help. The prop could not be placed by crane because of the overhang of the stern and special tackles had to be arranged by a rigger to get it from the ground up and under the overhang and in place ready to slide it on to the tailshaft. The rigger visited the site to size up where to put his lifting gear and on the appointed day the propeller, a beautiful bronze colour and a several tons in weight, was slowly hoisted into place and the propeller nut fitted and tightened with a massive spanner. A hollow cap was bolted over the large nut, about 24 inches in diameter, and then filled with molten tallow. The exterior part of the work was finished ready for the launch.

At the Caledon where there was a large expanse of river water available it was the practice to allow the propeller to rotate on launch under the action of being forced through the water. In other places e.g. the Clyde the propeller was held fast. The latter may have been done to assist in slowing the launch because of restricted free water on the Clyde. Drag chains were used on the Clyde but I never saw them used at the Caledon. At a launch in Dundee tunnel squad fitters would stay on board in the tunnel area to see that the tailshaft gland was working effectively.

After launch the ship would be caught and towed by tugs to the Boilershop jetty for further fitting out and the various trades would follow it there.

A launch day was a kind of festive occasion and it was always impressive to see a ship make its first move and slide into the river. There was usually a launch party comprising owners and management and I did check that the bottle smashed contained real wine. Members of the public could also get into the yard at a launch and on one occasion to my surprise my mother appeared.

The ship was caught in the river by tugs and taken to the Boilershop fitting out wharf.

The Boilershop wharf had a large crane which could lift 130 tons which was reputed to be the heaviest lift on the East coast of Scotland. This crane was necessary for lifting engines and other heavy equipment on board. A large motor ship engine could weigh 300 tons and was shipped in pieces usually two half bedplates, columns, entablatures or cylinders. A half bedplate and crankshaft for a B&W diesel engine could weigh about 90 tons.

The tunnel squad's job at the Boilershop jetty was to complete the assembly of the main shafting and to connect it to the main engine coupling. The shaft sections, usually made at Fife Forge in Kirkaldy, were shipped by the large crane and eased into place in the shaft tunnel which at this stage had a section of its top not yet in place in an aft hold. These sections were then fitted into the plummer block bearings and the shaft alignment checked before chocks were fitted under the plummer blocks.

The tunnel roof section was closed in and the shafting was approaching a state when it could be tested. The ship was moved east to the shipyard fitting out berth. This jetty was of recent construction being built by the Yorkshire Hennebique company in the early 1950's. I was to remain with the ship till the dock trials were over. Dock trials involved the powering up of the main engine, now connected to the shafting, alongside the wharf or jetty with the ship restrained by extra hawsers. These trials were carried out during the last stages of fitting out and allowed the quality of engine and shafting construction to be tested. One of the tunnel squad's last jobs on this ship was to assist in measuring the power transmitted by the shafting. A specialist firm's representative arrived and the fitters and I helped to mount the transducer round the mainshaft just inside the tunnel from the engine room. This device was a dynamometer or torsionmeter and had a transducer which measured the small angle of twist developed in the shaft which gave a measure of the torque transmitted. Used with the rotational speed the power could be calculated. This was the only time I ever received a gratuity which was in the form of a small cash sum for helping the visitor.

The main engine was a six cylinder opposed piston Doxford made in Sunderland and was a sight to behold when in motion with its upper crossheads rising and falling with little noise yet great majesty. The Doxford was the classic slow speed British designed and manufactured marine diesel engine.

The "City of Hereford" was approaching its sea trials phase and it was time for the tunnel squad to remove their gear and repair to their store.

The workload in a shipyard varied depending the progress of the ships' construction and fitting out. At quiet periods the squad would clear up the store and maintain and lubricate the boring-out machinery. The squad was unique in having its own handbarrow this being of being the two large wheel type.

I was given the job of greasing, and tidying this barrow up and arranged for the labourers to paint it in black enamel and I put some white lining out on the panels. I cleaned up and polished the brass wheel nuts so that they shone and flashed in the light as they rotated. There had never been a smarter wheelbarrow in the yard and as the lads pushed it through the yard much ribald comment was received about the "cartie" however they were up to it and gave their usual repartee.

I had wanted to work on the main engine squad from the start and my opportunity arrived. I said farewell to the tunnel squad, Shug Rogers chargehand, the screaming skull, the terrible twins, Sharpie, John McKew and the two Jims. I carried my toolbox to the Alfred Holt ship "Machaon" fitting out at the Boilershop. This initial main engine work was heavy with much slogging up of large nuts, in awkward corners, on large 2.5 inch bolts holding the fore and aft bedplate sections together. The main engine was a six cylinder Burmeister and Wain opposed piston diesel made by George Kincaid of Greenock. This was a massive engine about 50 feet long and 30 feet high with a normal running speed of 120 rev/min direct drive to the prop-shaft. The cylinder bores were about 750 mm.

There was certainly nothing very scientific about the work of the engine squad at this stage. The main parts of the engine were built slowly after a series of heavy lifts until all the main components were in place. These included the bedplate with crankshaft, columns, entablature, cylinders, lower and upper pistons. The skill here was in getting clean well aligned assembly of the component parts then achieving tight joints everywhere.

I was further engaged on fitting operating gear on to the engine of a lighter nature. Especially risky was working in the crankcase as heavy spanners and other parts would regularly be dropped from above sometimes without warning but hopefully an "Out below!" call was heard.

My journeyman was an ill tempered and impatient man so it was not turning out to be the pleasant job that I had expected. However the week was relieved by a day off to attend classes at the "Tech" in Bell Street.

College Days, Free time and Nick names.

I realised from the start that education was the key to progress. I therefore took the opportunity to attend Dundee Technical College, Bell St. to study for Ordinary and Higher National Certificates on a part time day basis. This meant one day off per week to attend college.

I had difficulty at first but soon got the hang of things and of an initial group of seventy plus who started the course I was one of the dwindling number who managed through to second year and ultimately to a fifth year class of about twelve.

The Head of department at that time was Mr Ferguson and lecturers during my course through the Department included Mr Sime, Mr John Main, Mr Fleming, Terry Doughty, John Milne, Jim Crabb and Dr G Robertson. They were a good bunch and were good teachers all. They saw through our group of students to fifth year which included a Bruce Ball prizewinner, several distinctions plus many special mentions and five of us went on to Glasgow to the Royal College of Science and Technology to study for the Honours Associateship which became the BSc Hons. But that was still in the future.

Arthur Jamieson won the Bruce Ball medal and Bill Fidler and I were so close runners up that we each received a proxima-accesit prize of solid silver propelling pencils.

The study programme comprised lectures, tutorials, drawing office work and lab sessions. This was a pattern which would continue at the Royal College (Strathclyde University). In third year at Dundee Tech a highlight in the laboratory programme was taking indicator cards on a two cylinder compound marine engine in the Heat engines laboratory. These cards allowed the "Indicated power" of the engine to be measured. The engine had been made by Gourlay Brothers of Dundee who were notable Engine builders and Shipbuilders. The firm had closed in 1908.

Leisure time for the apprentice could include snooker, the pictures (cinema), playing and/or watching football, the dance halls, drinking and the minority pastimes of fishing and hill walking. Snooker halls open in the 1950's included Maryfield, Imperial (High St.), Kings (Cowgate), Panmure (Wellgate), North End (Upper Hilltown), Clepington (Near Provost Road), Terrys (Brook St) and The Carse (Lindsay St). Dance halls available were the Palais (Tay St), Old Palais (Seagate), Empress (Dock St.), Robertsons (Hawkhill), Progress Halls (Lower Hilltown) and the Chalet Broughty Ferry. Terry's and North End were open on Sundays in an otherwise closed downtown Dundee. Terrys had a high counter and a row of time clocks for the tables. Terrys also had hot pies and tea for sale. I preferred the Maryfield Billiards saloon, the Palais in Tay Street, the Odeon cinema at Coldside , Greens in Nethergate and gave some time to supporting the Caledon Waverley football team.

It was in 1957 at the Palais Dancehall that I met Florence who would later become my wife. This relationship had a good effect on me and I took a renewed interest in my college studies. We continued as Monday evening dancers for some time enjoying the Music of the Andy Lothian band.

The nick-name culture in the shipyard is worthy of comment as there were some strange ones. The foreman in D shed was known as "the Knot" but this spelling is wrong since the reason he got the name was due to a practice of his while he was a chargehand on the ships fitting out. Empty gas bottles from the burners were to be craned ashore and he chalked on them

"Nought in bottles" Of course any person using such exotic language attracted attention and his name was created.

"Norrie the Op" was an engineering apprentice who had unwisely exposed in discussion his opportunistic plans for the future and paid the price. Discretion, I learned early, was the better path to tread.

An apprentice mis-read the word "Domestic" on a domestic fresh water tank which had a pillar in front of it showing the word as "dome stic" and had asked another what this meant. He was forever after known as the "dome stick".

A habitual borrower of tools was called "Johnny Geesalenno".

"The horse" was the name earned by a young fitter who was prone to work at a rather uncomfortable rate despite advice from his fellow fitters.

Another energetic fitter from Arbroath who moved about the engine-room rapidly was known as the "Fleein forky".

Riveter Bob Barty the Scottish Ballroom Dancing Champion was known as "Bob the Dancer". I was referred to as "British Railways" because of the woolen footplatemen's jacket I wore over my overalls.

A plater foreman was known as "the Mouse" and a ship manager of rounded appearance and hat was named "the Sputnik" this being contemporary with the Russian achievement in space.

The riveter foreman Alan Thomson was known Universally as "Po" Tamson. It was alleged that as a child he had got a chamber pot stuck on his head and hence the name. It did not help that he wore a large black bowler of similar shape.

The place was full of characters with a social texture unique to the shipbuilding background. I believe that there was a genuine comradeship present which grew out of a pride of workmanship and working together in harsh conditions.

One worker who stands out in my memory is Archie who worked outside on cleaning and grading the riveter's fire coke or char as it was known. One has to imagine a dark painfully cold winter's morning with hard frost on the ground. The coke was placed by Archie in a large sieve or riddle and submerged by hands in a tank of cold water where it was agitated by hand to wash it then the cleaned coke was thrown on to a pile. This was done to ensure a clean uniform char for the rivet heater boys' fires.

He was a mournful looking lean man of medium height in his late 50's but was stooped with his grinding toil. He wore a full length leather apron and was covered in the grime flying off the coke. His blackened nose had a perpetual drip at it and to me he depicted misery personified. I wondered as I passed on these bitter mornings how anyone could do such a task day in day out especially in these cold conditions. However he was a dedicated worker and it was said that Archie never had a day off. I heard some time later that he was told that he was to get a token of gratitude for long but continuing service with the Caledon company and he was asked what gift he would wish to receive. He answered " a new riddle".

Time on the Board

One morning while I was in the crankcase of the B&W diesel main engine on board the MV "Machaon" working on a valve actuating shaft "Big Jim" Blyth the ships engineering foreman sent for me to see him ashore in his office or "buckie".

His news for me was that I had been selected for drawing office training and that I should proceed for an interview forthwith. I was at this time in my third year "on the tools" and I had also been attending Dundee Technical College, Bell Street, with some success.

This was to be a return to the Engineering Drawing Office at the Boilershop in which I had spent my time as a print boy. This time however I would be working at a drawing board under the supervision of a senior draughtsman. The working hours were also more congenial with an 8.45 starting time. I would however lose some pay as a result of not earning PBR bonus.

The chief draughtsman in this office was Mr William McHardy with Bert Wallace as the second in command. I was assigned to work under Mr Kelso. The drawing bench was of the horizontal variety which allowed large rolled drawings to be worked upon. I was introduced to drawing on tracing paper with quite a hard pencil, usually 3H. Some draughtsmen used 6H which I claim etched rather than marked the paper.

The first job I was given was to draw the layout of holes in the tank top for Engine No 517 "Athel Prince" a molasses tanker.

This drawing was to be used on the actual ship by the "marker off" fitter who would measure up and mark on the ships tank top principal holes for services such as pipe entry fittings.

Ships engineroom drawings were categorised into the principal services e.g. fuel system, engineroom machinery arrangement, engine cooling system, refrigeration system etc. and would include funnel drawings and design of boilers if manufactured by the Caledon. A senior draughtsman would normally be allocated one of these systems and thence design and prepare the complete set of drawings for it.

This would include drawings of components and fittings which would be ordered from the manufacturing departments of the Shipyard or Boilershop. One could see the classic separation of deck and engineroom activities, the Boilershop being very much the Marine Engineering Department area.

For the first time I started to like engineering drawing. Like many things which one has to learn it is in the application of the knowledge that it gets to be more fun. I had to read the main fuel drawings and identify where a pipe penetrated the tank top and add the co-ordinates of the hole to my drawing together with details of the hole size. I had to check that the hole did not interfere with any structural beams or plates under the tank top.

Another apprentice job was the preparation of fitting sheets. I would get list of fittings for a pipeline and have to specify the flange thickness and hole layout and other details related to the service pressure and duty involved. This then formed the basis of an order to manufacture the valve and castings would be ordered, via the patternmakers, from an outside foundry. The Caledon did not have a foundry and castings would be bought in from places such as Dennyloanhead in Stirlingshire.

I also was required to design a daily service tank for oil fuel. This tank stored oil, pumped from the main fuel tank, for the diesel generators. This job entailed finding out how tanks were made

109

and what pads for fittings had to be included, manholes etc. The design when complete would be sent to Lloyds Register for approval and then for manufacture in the Boilershop.

Spare gear drawing was another apprentice job. This required the spare parts stowed in the engineroom to be listed and their position where stowed placed on the drawing. This was done when the ship was nearly ready for sailing on trials since the stowage positions were placed where room could be found and the drawing was a record for the ships engineer.

Drawing office apprentices were also roped in to help survey the use of insulation and cladding applied by the lagging contractor. A fellow apprentice Alan Boyd and I were detailed to assist a Mr Smith of the Dundee Boiler Covering Company to measure up the lagging placed by his company on a ship nearing completion. The ship in question was the "Baharistan" for the Strick line.

The job involved accompanying this Mr Smith and noting the area of lagging and its type and thickness on various parts of the engineroom equipment including engine exhaust pipes, boilers, tanks etc. A principal material used was asbestos but there was no warning of it being a dangerous material. The stuff would be falling like snow in the engineroom at some stages of the process including the time we were measuring up. This surveying was a somewhat tedious process and I was glad that I was only called to do it on one ship.

The best job of all which I experienced while in the drawing office was that of ships trials at sea. A selection of the draughtsmen who had worked on the ship were present as the ship's engineroom trials party.

The duties of the draughtsmen involved recording temperatures and pressures during sea trials to ensure that the systems were working as expected. One job in particular which I did was to record the starting air receiver (or tank) pressure as several engine starts were made. To explain, the large main two stroke diesel engine on these ships was started by compressed air at about 500psi. This air was introduced to the engine cylinders and pushed the engine round to build up momentum and then fuel was injected, ignition commenced and the engine ran.

This of course used up some of the stored compressed air in the starting reservoir and to satisfy Lloyds requirements there were limits set on how much the pressure fell with each start. This was why the loss in pressure had to be recorded. This operation was also witnessed by the Lloyds surveyor.

It was impressive to see the engine builder's representative's rapid start and stopping of the great Doxford engine with the accompanying scream of high pressure air entering the engine. It was also necessary to show that the engine could be reversed in a certain time. It was noted that the engine did not always reverse when it should have and there was a "wrong way indicator" fitted to alert the engineer to that fact.

I assisted a senior draughtsman Tom Elder on the trials of MV "Baharistan" both in the North Sea off the Tay estuary and off Blyth in Northumberland.

The Baharistan completed a short builder's sea trial before leaving Dundee to allow us and others to get the test equipment set up and tried out. This included thermometers and pressure gauges.

The main trials were to take place out of Newcastle to where the ship proceeded for dry-docking and bottom painting at Smith's Dock at North Shields.

On the eve of the appointed trials Tom and I travelled by rail to Newcastle where we stayed at the Sea Hotel in South Shields. This was a nice seaside hotel of 30's vintage of an architecture I have come to like very much.

We went out for a short visit after an excellent dinner to North Shields to see the ship. This required crossing by ferry and allowed me to see some of the shipping on the Tyne. In particular there was in dock a large whaling factory ship the "Southern Harvester" something that happily no longer exists.

South Shields was a nice resort town with a beach. North Shields was very much an industrial dockland with shipyards and large heavy industry and grey housing. However that was the sort of place that had made the real money all over Britain.

"Baharistan" was seen alongside the wharf at Smith's Dock looking wonderful and after a chat with the Caledon ship's manager we returned to our hotel for a night's rest prior to an early start on the trials day.

The ship had a large Doxford two stroke diesel main engine and high speed steam reciprocating engine generators. Some shipping lines preferred this mixed arrangement based on a belief that the reliability was better. I could not see the validity of this argument but in the Baharistan's case it had an energy saving quality in that the main engine exhaust passed through the steam boiler and therefore recovered waste heat for electrical generation. Combined heat and power (C.H.P.) has been applied in marine engineering for a long time.

The ship made for sea off Blyth on the measured mile and many tests were made during which we did our bit in recording performance. The only incident was when I was idly whistling on the half height flat of the engine gratings, waiting for the next instrument reading round, and several of the main engine builders men came running to see what was causing the gas leakage!

Whistling was not allowed because the sound was similar to a component about to seize or the sound of escaping high pressure gas. It is also believed to be unlucky to whistle on a ship.

After several hours of trials Tom and I were able to go to the splendid officers mess for a late lunch at sea. It had been a day of glorious weather and enjoyable work.

The ship cruised back up the Tyne to Jarrow and the trials party were disembarked to the waiting tug. As we pulled away from the ship in the atmospheric late red sky afternoon to return to Dundee Baharistan gave three long deep roars on its horn and the tug responded with its three toots.

It was a touching moment. Another fine Dundee built Caledon ship had joined Britain's Merchant Fleet.

We travelled up to Newcastle from Jarrow on the rattling electric train and boarded the next main line express for Dundee. It was a pleasant journey in the wood panelled LNER type bar saloon carriage of the train in the company of the other shipyard workers mainly riggers. The foreman rigger was Jim Middleton, no relation, a big likeable person who with his trials crew were good company. Until a ship is handed over to the owners it is operated by Caledon employees. Caledon engineers manned the engines and riggers and carpenters were the "seamen".

I continued in the drawing office learning new things and hearing many tales from the draughtsmen around me. There was a problem getting new orders in shipbuilding as the fifties drew to a close. It was not entirely clear to me why this was but it was probably based on the increasing Far East and German shipbuilding yards getting into their stride with well equipped shipyards and subsidies which lured away the British shipowners from their home yards.

The Caledon had taken steps in the mid 1950's to re fit the slipways with 15 ton cranes and the large pre-fab welding shop was producing the goods but ultimately competing prices out-bid the British yards. In Sweden considerable investment had been made especially in the Gothenburg yards and when I visited them in 1969 it was clear the management were a lively young crowd and the working equipment was impressive. They had also not had the same resistance to more efficient working practices that had been the case in the UK. Productivity was the key to survival and the methods to give greater productivity were not sufficiently present in the UK shipyards. There was a real need to apply production engineering principles to shipbuilding as the USA had done in World-War 2 but to apply these principles to produce high quality ships. Despite the Swedish efficiency measures their shipbuilding industry was to go the same way as that of the UK.

An excellent example of what could have been done was the building and fitting out of the "Vistafjord" at Swan Hunter's yard in 1974 where unitary construction was widely applied and the ship was delivered before time and to estimate. The Fairfield experiment in the 1960's also applied production engineering ideas to shipbuilding and with some success but this did not have the necessary government support to see it widely applied. What might have been?

There were understandable reasons for increased productivity to be resisted, after all the whole point was to produce more output for the same cost and this ultimately would mean less jobs in a yard of a given size. The labour unions did not see that following this resistive attitude was playing into the hands of the competitor. However, despite their admirable management even the Swedish yards would later have to close because of costs related to their standard of living, workers welfare and safety-at-work standards. These have to be compared to that of countries where these parameters were pursued with less zeal.

The situation was not yet obviously serious and the yard would continue for more than twenty years but my learning time was limited and I was considering other possibilities. The word was that the shipyard drawing office apprentices were working on "ghost" ships i.e. orders that had been cancelled and would never be built. This prospect did not appeal to me but was a logical step to train the designers of tomorrow.

Of the draughtsmen round me David Harley, Bill Bruce, Tom Elder and Charlie Donaldson would all take up teaching as a second career within ten years of 1959. No doubt they saw as I did that the writing was on the wall for shipbuilding in Dundee.

I asked Bill Bruce in 2003 how he felt the Caledon was a relatively successful yard given the casualty rate of other yards since the 1950's. He answered that for instance the Burntisland yard was like Woolworths and the Caledon was Fortnum and Masons.

The Caledon reputedly had higher standards of quality of build than many other yards and being a repetitive builder of ships for

115

Alfred Holt's Blue Funnel line must have helped to maintain that quality.

Training Pastures New – Precision Manufacturing

It was Autumn 1959; I was part way through my fourth year as an engineering apprentice with the Caledon Co. and I was making good progress with my studies in the Higher National certificate course at Dundee Technical College. Among my fellow students was an apprentice at Blackness foundry, Bob Meston, who had his apprenticeship transferred to Veeder-Root Ltd an American company making precision counting products. This transfer had been a result of the closure of Blackness foundry in 1958.

I was concerned that shipbuilding was going the same way and that there may not be a future in marine type engineering in Dundee. It was also an attraction to get experience in precision manufacturing engineering which was an industry prospering in the post war era.

I made enquiries of the training manager at Veeder-Root (VR) and an interview was arranged.

The Veeder-Root company had its HQ in Hartford, Connecticut USA and was one of several American companies to set up factories in the UK post second world war. The nature of the industry was precision manufacturing engineering which was generally called "Light engineering". This was a new industry to the Dundee area and involved the use of toolmaking and high productivity manufacturing techniques such as presswork, diecasting, electroplating, automatic turning machines and the like.

This was quite different from the heavy engineering business but the engineers involved required similar intellect and skills to do their job well.

The principal product line VR made at that time was the petrol pump computing head which was the mechanical device which calculated the cost of the petrol dispensed at a garage forecourt pump. This product comprised gears, shafts, hubs, bushes, frames, microswitches and many other parts. VR was particularly good at diecasting and was an industry leader in that technology.

The cycle mileometer was one of their earliest products which typified the precision of their finest diecastings. This type of product was their other main business i.e. small counters for industry. Their counters could be seen on many machines from diesel engines to textile machines, food machinery and indeed any place where an item had to be counted.

My interview was with Mr James Stephen the training officer and Quality Control engineer. Mr Stephen was a late thirties bespectacled formal sort of person in a white coat and conducted an interview along the usual lines of determining why I wanted to move away from the shipyard.

I suppose that I wanted to learn more of what might support me in the future and I said as much. I also met the chief engineer Mr A. Brough who was known to my colleagues at Caledon since he had worked there during WW2. This was another encouragement to me knowing that others had made the move into manufacturing.

I was given a works tour and could see something of the plant and the product. The visit finished with a medical examination.

I was in quite a quandary regards what to do for the best as this was not at all clear.

There was a stigma in "breaking one's time" though that term really applied to stopping an apprenticeship. What I was proposing was a transfer of my apprenticeship agreement from Caledon S&E to Veeder-Root Ltd with hopefully the agreement of both sides. I had discussed the matter with my father though he was not keen on moving my time. My elder brother Robert could see the sense in getting different experience but underlined the need to have it agreed all round.

There was still a glamour associated with the idea of "going to sea" and this was causing me some difficulty. I could see no glamour in working in a factory. However reality was getting the upper hand and previous concepts were being questioned. Did going to sea have more to do with sitting around in a cabin between engineroom watches longing for a return to home? This had seemed an acceptable future when a schoolboy or young apprentice but the comforts of home life were going to count for more in the long run. Nobody was positively encouraging me to go ahead but I decided that the change was for the best.

In due course I received an offer from Veeder Root to accept my transfer and they asked me back for a further talk to hear my further thoughts. At this meeting I stated that I wished to proceed. I notified the training officer at the Caledon that I had the offer to transfer and asked his advice. He did not stand in my way but did say that transfers usually went the other way with apprentices joining Caledon. This may have had something to do with conscription which was still in force. The Caledon training was a good one to have if one chose to do ones National Service in the Merchant Navy over 5 years. In my case it was looking like conscription would be over and new freedoms were possible.

After an interview with the Caledon Engineering director W.O.Gardiner, who was reluctant to agree but could see my reasoning, it was settled that I would start after New Year 1960 at Veeder-Root in the industrial estate at Dundee.

In retrospect this was a good move as it gave me an insight to how things are made in quantity to work well and reliably and at economic cost. This was the engineering which F. W. Taylor had used to make Henry Ford's fortune and which had swept the western world but mainly applied to light manufacturing industry including automobile manufacture. The management of people was also much different, and better, in this American industry. Heavy engineering labour relations were marked with adversity and dispute. The American management style was about co-operation to achieve production with quality and good pay with superannuation was received in return for fair work done in reasonable conditions. A principal difference was that good profits were being made by the business on a regular basis which in turn was a product of good management.

Time Transferred -over and out

I was to start a planned training at Veeder–Root in the factory which meant starting at 7.45am. Being January my first morning arrival was in darkness to a new environment, smells and noises. Timekeeping was strict and clocking on was required. I was placed under the supervision of one of the parts inspectors. The main factory areas were machine shops and assembly lines. The manufacturing system required parts to be made to specified tolerances and for example in the automatic turning machine section a %ge of these were checked as they were manufactured and their measurements plotted. Inspectors were usually engineering tradesmen i.e. ex-fitters or turners so I had a basis of common language with them. They had usually worked in engineering manufacture in or around Dundee e.g. Blackness Foundry, Sturrock & Murray, McLeans Engineering or Matrix at Brechin.

The machine shop environment was bustling, noisy and bee-hive like. Everyone seemed to have a job and be doing it and of course their bonus system was part of the management method. Automatic lathes, power presses, number wheel machines, diecasting machines, gearmaking and toolmaking could be seen from one physical standpoint.

A significant change from shipbuilding was the amount of women present. There were virtually no women in the shipyard workshops in my time but in VR the majority of the light production workers were female. They were mainly employed on repetitive tasks and most seemed to thrive on this work. The general noise level did not allow music to be played on the P.A. system.

Also there was an official tea break, morning and afternoon! Bear in mind that tea breaks were not officially allowed in the shipyard; another mark of the managerial chaos which prevailed there.

I quickly learned how to use a micrometer and also the important features of precision manufacture. I could see that some classes of turning machine could produce much closer tolerances than others and how these machines were best utilised. My training here would be to accompany the inspector for a machining area and see how dimensions and quality were monitored.

I was conscious of it being a closed environment in which to operate. One was not free to move around the factory without good cause and this was one of the oppressive things about factory work. But this was a freedom that had to be limited if labour was to be controlled.

I moved on during the ensuing months from lathes to drills to presses, gear-making, plating, diecasting and plastic moulding until all of the manufacturing processes had been covered.

The diecasting area was worthy of mention. In this area molten metal castings were produced on operator controlled Madison-Kipp casting machines in which molten zinc alloy was injected into a precision steel die. Many major parts of the VR products were made from castings of this kind. This could be dangerous work as sprayed metal stalactites bore witness.

One smaller casting machine which bore a date very early in the 20th century was automatic in operation and cast a metal known as Veedermetal. This cast a tin based alloy which could be moulded to very fine tolerance of size of the order of 1/10000 of an inch. It had been designed by the VR company in the USA and was used in the manufacture of castings for the small cyclometer type rev counter.

Aluminium casting started at VR Dundee for the first time while I was there. This produced stronger castings than the Zinc alloy used till then but was a slower process..

This was a time rich in learning and meeting many new people. With this kind of experience one could move to other major manufacturing industries with little trouble.

The next area in the factory to experience was the assembly lines. These included small counters and petrol pump counters. Small counters were a batch business and the environment was congenial and well paced. The petrol pump counter line was larger batch type assembly line, all male, and a vigorously paced operation. This production line was of course the principal money earner and where most of the action seemed to be.

However there was less to engage my attention in the assembly areas other than to witness what went on and what some of the problems might be.

This process took about six months and I was now to graduate to the drawing office.

There were two main drawing offices i.e. those of product design and tool design.

The product design office maintained the drawing collection for the company's products and these drawings had to be kept up to date with the latest modification and each product consist could then be known from time to time. This was important should spares become necessary for example.

Drawings of new products were also produced here but the effect of being a satellite factory could be seen in the fact that little if any new work was created in Dundee.

What normally happened was that products were conceived and decided upon at HQ in Hartford and made for the American market there. Such products that would suit the UK and its former colonies trading area had their drawings sent to Dundee for modification for the "English" market and to meet e.g. British Standards. This meant that the draughtsman at Dundee had a task of limited creativity and from my point of view the work seemed to be quite dull and largely "modification management". However I was there to gain an appreciation and make the best of it without complaint.

I was also conscious of a lower status enjoyed by these draughtsmen compared to those at the Caledon. At VR the charge draughtsman was a boorish rather rude person who did not appear to have come from the gentlemanly ranks of the drawing board.

The management method in the product design office was rather bullying-like and while I was there some draughtsmen were dismissed rather summarily at a quiet period. It was normal at VR for a staff person in these circumstances to be told to clear his desk within a few hours. This was rather shocking to me since I had taken these drawing office people to be reasonably secure staff types.

This was the other side of the coin of the high efficiency production machine.

However things were improving in other ways in that a new product was being designed to a different plan. A new petrol pump unit called a "Blender" was to be designed at VR UK at their offices at New Addington and Dundee engineering draughtsmen would be in attendance to create the production parts drawings from the concept drawings. The Blender controlled the mixing of different octane fuels. So new petrol pump product machine parts were being initially designed at Dundee i.e. Dundee had "Design Authority" This was a step forward in the status of the work and the drawing office.

I moved out of the drawing office about this juncture to spend periods in the time study, commercial and finance departments. This was to fill out my management experience and was much appreciated by me though my questions about profit and loss were not understood. I suppose like detail draughtsmen the accountancy clerks were not invited to comment on policy matters and were disturbed by such fundamental questions from an engineer.

The time study Department comprised two Methods engineers whose function was to measure the time taken to complete a task and record it. This information was then used to award a bonus to the operator for working faster than normal. For example one case I witnessed was the timing of the production of a turned part on a capstan lathe. The job was broken down into parts and operator was asked to execute the parts of the job while being timed with a stop watch. In addition to timing the work the Methods engineer was required to rate the work i.e. estimate if the person was working at normal rate or at a falsely slow or faster rate. Clearly the operator could contrive to make the job take longer than normal by performing slower under the stopwatch. The rating part of the job clearly required skill and experience.

This Department had to handle many enquiries from disgruntled operators from the shop floor regarding measured times and this was a tiresome task though in some cases the complaint would be justifiable.

In the commercial department I spent time with the shipping clerk and became aware of the wide range of places in the world to which the company's products were sent.

In the orders department invoices for parts and material ordered outside were reconciled with the delivery notes to check if the parts had been received in good quality and quantity. Payment was then made on the basis of good delivery.

The accounts department introduced me to the debit and credit ledgers and how these recorded the flow of money into and out of the factory.

My peripatetic existence was coming to a close and I would return to the drawing office to take up engineering duties. This time I went to work in the Tool Design section. Tool Design is necessary to provide the special tooling required to support the economic and efficient production of precision machines. The Toolroom would make tools to these designs to very high accuracy. In high quantity production the age of the craftsman-hand-made product had disappeared in the mid 1800's mainly due to developments in the Eastern manufacturing states of the USA. Parts now had to have their accuracy made by machine and this in turn gave rise to the need for high accuracy machine tools and jigs and fixtures to use with these machine-tools. This was the "Light engineering" industry which Scotland so seriously required as its heavy industry declined. It had been present in some UK places e.g. Singers in Glasgow and Ferranti in Edinburgh and in the Midlands and South of England.

My first task in the Tool Design office was to design a simple drill jig to allow an operator to drill a few holes in exact places on a part. "Exact" has no real meaning of course since nothing can be made exactly but only within a prescribed margin of error or "tolerance". This was an enjoyable task since it had a stated requirement and I could ask for help to achieve the aim. Essentially the part was to be held on locating pins in a fixed position and bushes provided to guide the drill to position. My job was to design this device and make drawings for the tool to be made by the Tool-room.

The Tool Design team had much more freedom of action in what they did than the Product designers and this seemed to come over in their spirit and actions.

I stayed several months in this section employed in several challenging tasks but was ordered back to the Product Design section because they needed people there temporarily.

Time marched on and the end of my apprenticeship was in sight. During the five years of my apprenticeship I had been following the National Certificate courses at the Dundee Technical College Bell St which was a Central Institution of the Scottish Education Department. I have to give the address because several institutions have used the description but at that time the premier part time technical education institution was "the Tech" Bell St and its National Certificate courses led to membership of the leading professional Engineering Institutions.

I had been doing reasonably well in the courses and was now approaching the Higher National Certificate final examinations. These were passed with distinction and I applied to join the third year of the four year full time Engineering Associateship course at the Royal College of Science and

127

Technology Glasgow (RCST). At this time only the Universities could award degrees and higher Engineering education was provided in superior technical colleges such as Imperial College, London and the Royal College of Science and Technology (RCST) together with other places such as Salford and Heriot Watt Edinburgh. The qualification at RCST was the Associateship of the College i.e. ARCST.

This was the plan and Veeder Root in the person of the Managing Director Peter Williams kindly offered me employment during my vacations during the course.

I also benefited from the then recently introduced student grant scheme which gave a good level of grant to pay fees allow study away from home. The grant amounted to about £10 per week (untaxed) for 32 weeks. I had been working as a junior draughtsman at VR for about £12 per week before tax and insurance.

I finished my apprenticeship in August 1961 and worked on for a short time at VR till I left to start my studies at the Royal College of Science and Technology in Glasgow in September.

DM Apprentice 1958

Florence, London 1959

Caledon Boilershop ca 1950 (photo Scottish Aviation)

Caledon Stannergate Yard 1956 (photo J D Forbes)

See image credits p267

MV City of Hereford 1958   (photo J D Forbes)

Mv Machaon 1959   (photo J D Forbes)

See image credits p267

Boilershop –not Caledon – a Vancouver Yard Scotch Boilers

MV Constance Bowater 1958   (photo J D Forbes)

MV Constance Bowater 1958   (photo J D Forbes)

Main Engine top platform- Kincaid marine diesel engine

(photo Temple Press)

See image credits p267

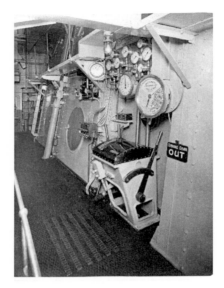

Main Engine starting platform-Scott Doxford   (photo Bedford LeMere)

Veeder Root petrol pump Variator

Veeder Root small Counter

Part 3 1961 to 1964

Higher Education

I had achieved a good result in the Higher National examination at Dundee Technical College (Bell St.) leading to an IMechE prize and a special college prize for "Outstanding performance". There was an opportunity to continue studies at the Royal College of Science and Technology (RCST) Glasgow (now Strathclyde University) for the qualification of Associateship of the College. This was of Engineering Degree standard and could be awarded at Honours level. This would start in September 1961 and was to be direct entry to the final two years of a four year course. This direct entry allowance was the big attraction to apply to RCST as e.g. Queens College Dundee of St Andrews University had no such allowance at that time. I had been in the short leet for the Bruce Ball medal along with Bill Fidler and Arthur Jamieson but Arthur won the medal and Bill and I received a special "proxime accessit" prize of an engraved solid silver pencil.

My apprenticeship had finished in August 1961 and the Veeder Root Company kindly offered to employ me till I started at RCST and in the vacations during the course. A fellow employee Bob Meston was also to study at RCST and received the same terms at VR.

The first hurdle in preparation for RCST was to arrange accommodation in Glasgow.

Arthur Jamieson took a group of us to Glasgow in a car and we followed up replies to an advert he had placed in the paper there. I was to share with Norman Mathieson from Tomintoul at digs in Sims Hill to the Southside of Glasgow near Cathcart.

The first impression of RCST was of its large size occupying its imposing site on George Street and North to Cathedral Street. Engineering was housed in the modern Weir building in Montrose Street.

The lecture programme at RCST would follow the normal pattern we had become accustomed to but on a larger scale. The lecture room atmosphere was different though in that respect for the lecturers was much lower than at Dundee. There was seemingly a culture of disrespect for authority and a spirit of revolt among the largely Glasgow students but in a humorous childish way. For example if the lecturer made a minor mistake in a calculation on the blackboard there would be a loud stamping of feet till the error was corrected. There would be other pranks such as setting a hidden alarm clock to go off during the lecture or pulling the blinds and switching off all the lights before the lecturer came in. In that instance the lecturer entered and proceeded to lecture in the pitch dark till someone switched the light on. This sort of behaviour was accepted by some of the staff but others were very stern and would have no nonsense.

Overall I found the course to be hard work with little feeling of collegiate spirit but that is what we had become used to. There were other direct entry HNC types like us in the class from industry round Glasgow including shipyards and steelworks.

The programme of studies comprised the usual pattern of lectures in the mornings and laboratories or drawing offices or more lectures or examples classes in the afternoon five days a week.

Glasgow at this time was a gritty black city before the introduction of the clean air act and the iron and steel works of the Clyde valley would pour out pollution on a large scale. This was most evident during the winter fogs which were a choking murky yellow atmospheric obscenity present everywhere outdoors and in. It was little wonder there was so much respiratory disease in the city.

It is difficult now to identify anything remarkable about the course other than a feeling of grinding emergency. As direct entry students we had to catch up in several areas of study notably mathematics, electrical engineering and chemistry and this required extra hours of work. The chemistry lectures were difficult to follow as much was assumed and not explained. Chemistry laboratories on Friday afternoons were chaotic affairs with each student pursuing their own experiments with titrations proceeding wrongly, flasks boiling over and bursting, H_2S leaking from the fume cupboards where students were percolating a solution to produce a precipitate and weird results experienced in the balance room. Supervision was minimal or absent and one was supposed to know for example that caustic was the same stuff as sodium hydroxide. This took place at a time on Friday when we east coast types wanted away to catch the 5 o'clock train at Buchanan Street station for our weekend at home. We learned the hard way. A good standard textbook would have helped at this time but that was not the method in use. Lectures were the thing and you were expected to understand all that was necessary from them. Luckily chemistry was the poor exception and laboratory work in other subjects was better understood.

The Mathematics course was a major hurdle even with provision made for the direct entry students. The degree of difficulty experienced was of course a personal thing and some students walked it. Others like myself struggled with the pure mathematics course especially in calculus. Statistics was followed much better and did have a clearer application.

General studies was an enjoyable interlude and was well presented by an able group of lecturers who encouraged us to challenge accepted norms. These lecturers included e.g. historians, economists and English Language types. Work still had to be done however on assignments. One name that was to become familiar in later years of historical study was one Butt; another younger man had been present at the Hungarian uprising and commented upon it.

Electrical engineering was very well presented and we were fortunate to have Dr Tedford lecture the course. This was intensive and thorough and a course with which I had little difficulty.

The third year comprised two three-month terms followed by a six month vacation. This reflected the applied nature of studies at RCST and one was expected to work in engineering employment during the vacations which made the VR offer most welcome.

Third year was overall a tough struggle but we were brought up to speed and prepared for the final year.

Lunch was taken in the Student Union which was a newish building in John Street. This provided many facilities for the students including quiet study areas, a ballroom, a cinema, bar and most important a large canteen. There was also a floor solely for female students called the "Muirhead".

Films were shown every day at 1pm in the cinema. These were always Fred Quimby cartoons and were greeted by the audience with shouts of Fred! Fred!

Apart from these cartoons films were shown some Wednesday afternoons but we engineers seldom had the free time to see them. We had a busy timetable of afternoon laboratory attendance and some lectures.

The lodging at Sims Hill had not lasted as transport was limited and I found sharing a study/bedroom did not suit me. I moved to a room in a typical third floor red sandstone Glasgow flat in Cathcart Road near Crosshill station on the Cathcart circle line. Public transport here was plentiful, trolley buses and trains, and suited me fine. Louie and Bella Ellis were the middle aged Jewish proprietors and we got along tolerably well for the rest of that academic year.

I visited friends at the officer's quarters at Barlinnie prison on a couple of occasions. Jim Band had been a patternmaker at the Caledon when I was there in the 1950's. Barlinnie was a grim place but the officers' social club did a very nice ham soup which I sampled with relish. I just made the last bus from Barlinnie which terminated at Parkhead cross far short of the city centre where I would catch the trolley bus for Cathcart Road. Parkhead was a grey dark tenement area with youths lurking in shop doorways up to no good and generally misbehaving. I was glad to board an approaching rickety tram making its way into the city. Trams and trolley buses seemed to keep running later than the buses.

I would travel home with my fellow east coast types to Dundee at weekends on the train service from Buchanan St Glasgow to Dundee West station and this was a good service in the main. Still mainly steam hauled; Standard Class 5 locos, A3 and A1 were common motive power. A4s were running the Aberdeen express trains via Forfar. Recent 2nd class compartment stock gave a comfortable journey and this was a social journey when we could talk about things without the rush and tumble of college life.

After the third year finals were over I returned to Dundee and took up the offer of employment at Veeder Root. This was to be in the Drawing office which had moved into the new North

141

extension. This was a large open plan office then in fashion and based on the American style in which all departments shared the same large office space. There were good views of the Sidlaws and plenty of light permeated the place.

I was allocated to work on tool design and plant layout.

One project at that time was tool design work comprising the preparation of design drawings of casting dies and press tools for new products. Poor quality drawings of the American factory's dies had been sent over and required minor alteration. It was essentially a copy job to provide more legible drawings to be sent out to tool suppliers. The work was not very challenging and there was no scope for creativity whatsoever. Some tools would be made in house in the VR toolroom but when a new product was planned the bulk of the tools were bought in.

There were plans afoot for new production machinery and a model was being prepared of the factory layout. This layout was largely under the control of Andy Brough the chief engineer of the Dundee factory. It was not clear to me why such a model was required for this particular layout but it was probably the fashionable desire of USHQ. Basically it was a good idea but expensive relative to the usual practice of plant layout drawings which were prepared anyway.

But it was a paid job in industry and there was always some morsel of learning picked up.

The main petroleum product was the petrol pump computer in its various forms. This was a purely mechanical device comprising many diecastings and the version popular at the time was the "Blender". This allowed a pump to dispense a blend of two different petrol octane types and calculated the price accordingly.

142

This was prior to the introduction of electronic instruments which would follow in the 1970's.

Electronics in the early 1960's was still valve (Thermionic) based and voltages around 200 to 300 volts were required. This limited their use anywhere near inflammable vapours. Later in the decade amplifiers using voltages of the order of 9 volts would be introduced and when, in the 1970's, used in conjunction with microcomputers would revolutionise counting instrumentation.

Other draughtsmen in the office at that time were Jim Brown and Hamish Winters both tool design types. On the product design team were Albert Barclay and Angus Langlands. Veeder Root had at this time 1961-2 invested in new large diecasting machines which allowed Aluminium diecasting as opposed to their usual Zinc alloy diecasting.

In July 1962 Florence and I Married at Baxter Park church and we honeymooned at Aberdeen.

I had failed the Maths exam in March in common with many others including Bob Meston and Arthur Jamieson in that year but after due diligence I passed the re-sit in August.

Honours Year 1962-3

In September 1962 the summer vacation came to an end and preparations were made to Return to the Royal College. I put an ad in the Glagow evening times for a flat and from the replies chose to visit one in Queens Drive overlooking Queens Park. This was in a four storey "good "tenement with a tiled close. The flat was a large 7 room one with an upstairs. The room on offer was smallish with its own locking door and looked to the rear of the building but was adequate for my purposes. There was an electric fire, a baby Belling cooker, a card table, chest of drawers and a single bed (bring own linen). I was informed by the proprietor Mrs English that the room next door was occupied by Lord Erskine Murray (whom, it turned out, was very rarely there).

I would get minor groceries on my way back to the flat in the evening after I had tea in the student's union in John Street. My diary records a typical purchase of Corn Flakes, brown bread, digestive biscuits, chocolate digestive biscuits, quarter pound of butter, tea bags and 10 Consulate (cigarettes), total cost 7/6. I also note that my trouser measurements were 33inch leg 31inch waist.

On the evening of 14th February 1963 I attended the Mechanical Engineers' dinner and smoker which was a grand affair. The main dish was trout. The speaker was a man called Gray who gave an entertaining talk related to the removal of the Stone of Destiny from Westminster Abbey. He produced from his pocket a small piece of stone which he claimed was from the great stone itself.

I liked the lodgings set up as it was near to Victoria Road which was a pleasant shopping area. Public transport was readily available with regular trolley buses and trains into the centre of Glasgow. The rent included a supply of corn flakes. Strange, but this had something to do with the law on rented rooms. If food was supplied there was some lesser payment to the council or to tax.

I duly turned up at Queens Drive upon the appointed day at start of term with my bedding and books ready for the signing on process at the Royal College which comprised waiting in a long snaking queue and signing up for the new session.

This was fourth year which would comprise six months of study with final exams in March 1963 and if performance had been adequate a further three months of project work for honours.

Students had to choose five main subjects which would have attendant laboratory sessions. The subjects I chose were Thermodynamics, Technical Dynamics and Control, Mechanics of Fluids, Nuclear Power Engineering. Industrial Administration and General Studies were compulsory.

The Professor of Mechanical Engineering was Adam Thomson but we rarely met him.

This was a more enjoyable year than third which had been something of a sweat shop.

Classes were still large and of the order of 30 in two streams. Classes were held Monday to Friday all day with no Wednesday afternoon off as in other Institutions of higher education. Final examinations were held in March and I attained sufficient marks to be invited back for Honours which entailed conducting a laboratory based project full time.

About this time I saw an advertisement in the press inviting applications for an engineer post at the British Aluminium (BA) plant at Kinlochleven. I applied in case the Honours option did not result and I was later invited for interview. This was timed for a Saturday in late March and I set out by train from Dundee West station to Dunblane where I joined the Glasgow-Oban train via Callander. I left the train at Tyndrum where a BA car was waiting for me. The car travelled by way of Glencoe and it was snowing. I met the chief engineer and the personnel officer there and following an interview I was shown the works. The main activity was the reduction of alumina to make aluminium metal. Electric current was passed through molten alumina. This process employed many Pelton wheel turbine driven generators. Much of the job was to be involved with the production of graphite components for the production process which looked to be carried out in a rather black environment. This graphite production facility had been used to make the core components for the early UK nuclear power stations. I was left to have a lunch in the canteen and I looked out the window to a mountain surround under a grey sky. I felt that this was a mature process and not an environment which would allow me to experience cutting edge engineering. This decided me against the job but I wanted to keep my options open should no honours option resulted. I thanked the Chief engineer for the visit and said I would let them know. My trip back to Dundee was via the Bedford Duple service bus to Tyndrum hotel where I took a nice tea before joining the train for Dunblane and home. Days later I received the invitation for Honours and I wrote to BA declining their kind offer.

My honours project involved designing and making an electrical analogue of a controlled process plant. This was to allow a study of the modelled plant to various operating conditions. Such analogues were popular at that time which was before the age of general application of digital computers.

This project was a good introduction to technical electronics which would be useful in future employment.

So what to do next? There was a scheme of interviews run by the Careers office of the Royal College. I applied to Shell Oil and had a good interview with an experienced practical oilfield engineer who must have been satisfied with the interview as I was moved to the next level of the process. This was held at the then new Shell centre in London South bank. This was a very large building and I had detailed instructions (very necessary) on how to find my interview room. The interviewer this time was an early 40's man of rather stiff superior manner and not very sociable. I was to experience this type in other places of work and a common denominator in them was a private sector English education. While I experienced this attitude in four people in diverse places there were exceptions. My wish at the time was to get into process industry and in particular heavy oil and chemicals production. I had liked my work in marine engineering and I thought that petrochem would be similar. Anyway the man thought that Carrington Oil Refinery at Manchester would be the place for me and he said that he would arrange for me to be seen there by appointment. I was cooling towards this scenario as I had an image of living in a bungalow in some foreign country eg Arabia.

As it happened the letter informing me of the appointment came with quite short notice and would clash with examinations. I had to refuse the appointment and this was viewed dimly and that was the end of that opportunity. As things would turn out I had not missed out as other opportunities would arise.

The next college based interview was for ICI. We had had a presentation from a man in a lecture type situation and I filled in a form and submitted it then. I received an invitation to the ICI plant at Runcorn in Cheshire. There were several plants there engaged in the manufacture of Chlorinated Hydrocarbons. An example of this was dry cleaning fluids and other solvents and chemicals used in the manufacture of e.g. paints and plastics. Phosgene, ie mustard gas, had been made there earlier in the century.

This was not a pretty environment but a wealthy one. It was a low lying heavily industrialized area with grim looking smoking industrial plants.

I travelled from Glasgow to Runcorn via Crewe and got a taxi to a staff house called Lindsay House. This was a rather nice hotel-like residence exclusively for ICI personnel and visitors. I had a nice meal and a single room with facilities. After tea and settling in we

147

were addressed by a "rather nice" chap from personnel whom I would now describe as a medium height smartly sports jacket dressed liberal arts graduate (camel waistcoat, brogues) from Oxbridge. We then proceeded to a grand dinner followed by brandy and cigars. This was more like it. We could then socialize, play snooker or watch television. Drink was liberal and free. This may have been part of the screening process to see what bad habits became evident. Alcoholic drinking was an unhealthy pastime with many students and would be a negative indicator.

I was woken next morning at 7:30 by a servant with a cup of tea. The only time in my life this has happened. After breakfast we met with officers of the company. We had an introductory talk with slides, visited the plant and offices and were then interviewed individually. There were two suited capable middle management men probably engineers and they conducted a searching interview sat side by side on the other side of a desk. I did not do this well and did not feel that I had given of my best. I am not sure to this day just what they were looking for but it was almost as though one had to say that I had been waiting all my life for a job in a place like this.

It had been a good experience and helped me to sort out my preferences for workplace. I travelled back to Glasgow via Liverpool with other Scottish based applicants and we had dinner on the train at ICI expense in a cosy plush LMS type dining car. An offer from ICI did not ensue for me or the other Royal College types.

There should have been a greater sense of urgency but there was not. However another option reared its head. There had been a path trodden to the Royal College from Dundee which I and others had taken. There was now another path evident: that of studying for an MSc in Thermodynamics at University of Birmingham. Other Dundee students Bill Fidler and Arthur Jamieson had made this decision and I applied too. I was successful in my application and applied for a grant from the Department of Industrial Research (DSIR). The grant available was reasonably generous and after discussion with my wife I decided to proceed to Birmingham. This was done in the belief that it would open more doors to careers. It was also an area of study which I preferred and would be prepared to work in.

Meanwhile work on the project continued mainly in the Dynamics Laboratory in the Weir building in Montrose Street Glasgow under the nominal supervision of lecturer Mr Reid. I was assisted in making the analogue by James Sey a senior technician in the Electronics workshop. Much stories were dispensed and I learned that he had spent an apprenticeship with the famed Halley fire engine company of Paisley. I proceeded to testing the analogue and writing up the results for my Honours thesis.

This period of study was completely different from the usual lecture, tutorial, exams routine of the undergraduate world. There was now time to relax some evenings rather than the solid evening study work of the preceding years. Bob Meston, Bill Fidler and I had several evenings on the Queens Park putting greens during the summer of 1963.

One evening we bought a bottle of wine and played music in my room. We borrowed the record player from nurse occupants in the flat. Mrs English was not amused and told me so.

We also attended concerts of the Scottish National Orchestra then performing in temporary premises in the Kelvin Hall; one example was a memorable performance of Ravell's Bolero conducted by

Alexander Gibson. I also visited the cinema in Sauchiehall St to see Lawrence of Arabia on its first release.

One afternoon we three travelled on the Blue Train to Balloch on Loch Lomond where a boat was hired and a couple of hours enjoyed bobbing around the loch edge.

The Honours project came to an end in August 1963 and was written up in preparation for typing and binding. I had a false start getting it typed but I located a professional typist in Dundee via an ad for book authors. She lived in Downfield Dundee and made a good job of it. I took the typescript to Burns and Harris who bound it but were unhappy with the size of the margins, anyway it was too late to change and it was duly bound. Bill Fidler and I travelled to Glasgow to submit the theses and cleaned out our lockers thus finishing at Strathclyde, bar the graduation which would take place in December 1964.

University of Birmingham 1963-64

Bill Fidler and I had heard of a residence at Birmingham for post-grads called Chad Hill. I applied for a place there and was successful as was Bill and we would be sharing a room. Chad Hill was a Georgian mansion situated in Edgbaston overlooking Chad valley. (So that's where the toymaker got its name). This mansion sat in its own grounds with a lodge house and driveway. Buses passed this way heading for the University some 1.5 miles distant near the area of Selly Oak.

The day, a Saturday to allow time to settle in, came for us to travel to Birmingham a journey which entailed travelling by train to Edinburgh Waverley, and boarding the Edinburgh to Birmingham New Street train. Edinburgh Caledonian Station was still in use but at weekends the Birmingham trains left from Waverley. It

150

seemed a long journey to Birmingham where we arrived at about 4pm. New Street had an underground feel to it being quite black in colour and lacking natural light. We then emerged into Corporation Street to see the navy blue and cream city buses. But we had cases so this once it would be a taxi to Edgbaston.

Arriving at Chad hill we entered and looked for some reception desk. The place was deserted but eventually a Canadian resident came along and welcomed us saying that being Saturday few staff were available but to set down our cases and have a look round till teatime. The housekeeper would then be able to show us our room.

We had a look at the garden which was mostly lawn but with a dilapidated greenhouse and somewhat overgrown shrubs and trees. There was a good range of Rhododendrons though not in flower at the time.

The public rooms on the ground floor included a lounge, overlooking the lawn via French windows, of couches and easy chairs and a small library, a TV room with couches, a billiard room with a full size table and, via a conservatory passage, the dining room with two long refectory tables. The main house had large bedrooms upstairs comprising three rooms overlooking the garden and two other bedrooms.

The large bedrooms were each shared by two residents. There was to the rear what would have been the staff part of the original house with small bedrooms on three floors. A modern, probably 1950's, extension completed the residence adding about ten more rooms including the wardens flat. There was a set of five lockup garages in addition.

The original house had been owned by the Chance family of glass fame and had been rented since the mid 1950's by the University as a male postgraduate student residence with a high proportion of international types.

When we got to our room it was to find a large twin bedded room overlooking Harborne Road and the Chad Valley with the Edgbastion treed area reaching off into the Southern distance. There was a fireplace with a gas fire and the luxury of a second small room, probably a dressing room in the original house. It looked to the west in the direction of Chancellors hall.

The housekeeper advised us about mealtimes and being Saturday a cold meal was provided. Generally half board was provided with lunch at the weekends with a cold afternoon tea. This was cold meats and cake with tea or coffee. Bill and I went out after tea for a walk to the University and a first look at the Department building.

The Mechanical engineering building was red brick of modern design maybe 1940s to 1950s. As we would learn later there was a history of Thermodynamics excellence dating from Professor Mucklow's time when much of the Thermo labs would have been developed. The Department ran a one year MSc in Thermodynamics and Related studies which was the course we had opted for.

We met our fellow residents over the weekend and there were graduate students from many parts of the world. The bachelor warden Bill Gibson was a zoologist lecturer and was ex Indian Army so as one would expect he was a moustached military type but with a good measure of humanity. He addressed us all on Monday evening and laid down the house rules.

152

Sunday breakfast was later than in midweek and there was good range of heavy Sunday papers. Sunday lunch was English style , usually a roast and sweet at about one o'clock. Afternoons could be spent walking or getting some coursework done. Letters home were written on Sunday morning.

A good bus service to the University ran from the bottom of the Chad Hill drive followed by a walk over the railway and canal. The lecture room for the "Thermo" MSc programme was located in the Department and this would be the base for all courses. It was on the second floor of the Mechanical Engineering building and it had stool seating at bench type tables.

The format was familiar to us and included lectures, tutorials and laboratory work.

While Wednesday afternoon was free for sporting activity or private study classes were held on Saturday mornings.

Lunch was taken in the student Refectory which was a recent 1960's building with a large airy dining room. Menus were reasonably good and we did see new dishes such as paella but no Scotch pies and beans which had been a staple at Strathclyde.

The class comprised students from a wide variety of background and national origin. There were five Scots, an anglicised Pole, 5 Canadians, a few from the Indian Continent, a Turk, a Cypriot, an Iraqui, and seven Englishmen.

As on any course the routine sets in and there is the daily programme of lectures, tutorials and labs. During a lecture one could hear the industrial life of Birmingham going on in the background. There was a drop forge running somewhere with its heavy low frequency thump; shotgun fire from the gunsmiths works in Selly Oak.

153

A relief from the grind was provided by an excursion to the Motor show 1963 at Earls Court London. The wide range of mostly British made cars was admired during the leg wearying visit. The fastest car in the show was said to be the latest Rolls Royce costing £8900. Other makes were the Hillman Imp (made in Scotland), Rover 2000, lookalike Triumph 2000, Austin VanDenPlas 1100, Vauxhall Viva, E and S type Jaguars and 2 litre Morgan to name a few. After the show we grabbed a cheap meal of fish and chips in a café and had a quick visit round London central area including the British Museum, Piccadilly and finally Soho. I developed an abdominal pain that evening which remained during the night run back to Birmingham. I visited the University Doctor next morning after a disturbed night and he prescribed Librium after satisfying himself that it was nothing serious. In fact this was a critical point and I almost left the course. Strangely several others on the course were also wondering if it was the right thing to do and a few of us sought opinion from Prof Bannister. It seems three or four weeks into a course away from home leads to feelings of depression and I guess that was part of the problem.

Anyway we settled down and got on with things and there was the trip up to Scotland in late November to look forward to, by the Royal college students, for our graduation. Arthur Jamieson arranged the hire of a Ford Zephyr 6 Mk3 car and we set out on a cold dark morning. The Motorways were partly in operation and we were able to use the M6 for a short way then it was down to ordinary roads through villages and towns, traffic lights and slow moving heavy trucks. The Lancashire traffic police in their smart MG sports cars were seen. Stewart McRobert was dropped off at Dalbeattie and I dismounted just opposite Florence's home on the Kingsway Dundee.

Florence, my sister Nancy and I travelled to Glasgow on the Saturday for the Royal College graduation which was held in the assembly hall in the old building in George Street. Graduands were processed as usual climbing up to the stage and being presented to Lord John Reith of BBC fame. We later had a nice lunch at Lewis's in Argyll St. After a nice weekend in Dundee the student trip back to Birmingham was achieved without mishap and our studies resumed.

Bill Fidler and I travelled North again to Dundee at the end of term for the Christmas vacation. We boarded the busy overnight Edinburgh train at New Street and sat up with other passengers smoking while we tried to get some sleep. There was a change at Carstairs early in the morning to the Edinburgh train into Edinburgh Caledonian station at the Western end of Princes Street situated behind what is now the Caledonian hotel. There was then a walk the length of Princes Street to Edinburgh Waverley and the Dundee train.

I had bought an old 1937 Standard 9 in August and Florence and I had had a good holiday using it to tour around. This had been put off the Road when I left for Birmingham and I now brought it out for the Christmas vacation. This was something of a mistake as I found that the engine did not like cold conditions of running and would conk out after ten minutes or so. The reasons were probably connected to the worn state of the engine and much time was spent trying to fix the problem.

I had to set about a study of my academic work because there were term examinations to be sat on our return to Birmingham in January.

Bill and I returned to Birmingham on a cold Sunday on 5th January 1964 during the Aberdeen Typhoid epidemic. Being

Sunday we had to travel via York where the Railway operators contrived to send off the Birmingham train as the Edinburgh – London train arrived. This meant a four hour wait in York till the next train.

We left Dundee at 10.22 am and arrived at Birmingham at 20.30.

The top pop tunes at this time were the Beatles "She Loves You", "All My Lovin" and "Money". And by others "Hippy hippy shake" and "Glad all over".

There was some nervousness at Birmingham about us Scots arriving from the Aberdeen direction but there were no sanctions and no illness experienced.

With the term examinations over the next term was tackled. This was a more tractable term of work and there was improving weather after February. Birmingham lies 750ft above sea level and it experiences some harsh winter conditions and the thickest fog I had seen.

The second set of examinations were completed in May and I felt better about them than those earlier. I sat an oral in the subject of Thermodynamics and that completed the requirements for the degree but there was a project to do in the summer term.

I did this project work in a group with Arthur Jamieson and a Canadian Les Crosthwaite.

Meanwhile at Chad Hill things were settled down and we had enjoyed some social events.

There was the Christmas Dinner followed by lounge games. This I suspected would become a drunken brawl based on what I knew about officers mess games. It was. I managed to avoid the "Tunnel game" which comprised setting up two couches on their face forming a tunnel; the two teams then endeavoured to reach the other end – at the same time. One chap suffered a broken arm. Enough said.

There were also a couple of "At Home" evenings when guests, usually academic staff, were invited to dinner and drinks. These were enjoyable affairs and the food was markedly improved that evening.

One tradition was the annual Sunday afternoon Lacrosse game in March against the lady students of Chancellors hall. I was somehow dragooned on to this potential farce but was pleased when heavy rain meant the match was cancelled. A nice tea with a darts and snooker competition took place instead.

An enjoyable car based treasure hunt took place one June Sunday evening and Bill and I joined a car owing fellow resident to drive around the SW side of Birminham looking for clues such as , at Alvechurch, "Erithacus Rubecula" at the war memorial.

The answer was a soldier with the name Robin.

Arthur Jamieson, who lived in a rented bungalow in Northfield, was to spend a week away with his family and kindly offered me the use of his Jowett Javelin (flat four engine and aluminium body) while he parked it at Chad Hill. Bill and I travelled down to Stratford on Avon for the day and enjoyed visiting the town and the arrangements in place for Shakespeare's 400th anniversary. I took a wrong turning at one point and managed to drive on to the racecourse.

The time at Birmingham had been mostly enjoyable and more like what a University experience should be. The campus was pleasant, the student union which was in an Elizabethan style building was congenial and new things were learnt. However the separation from Florence was a problem and we had, early on in the academic year, discussed the possibility of her coming to Birmingham and us taking a flat. I had visited the flat of a fellow married student who had taken a flat for the year with his wife who sought work in Birmingham. The flat was very basic in a grim area of the city and not at all appealing. Florence would have to work in alien environment with new workmates and I would have to have study facilities or work at the University in the evenings which would mean she was left on her own a lot. It did not seem workable so we carried on with the present arrangement. I was conscious of the fact that had I stayed at Caledon till I finished my HNC I would have gone to sea and been away quite a lot so what I was actually doing was more home based and would hopefully result in a the MSc degree.

I was looking for a job during the summer term and had sent off several applications. I also noted that there was a Student Appointments Service and sought an interview.

The appointments officer, it turned out, was the brother of the actor Peter Hordern.

The Service occupied rooms in concrete huts near the University playing fields and I turned up at the appointed time for my interview with him. I found him an unpleasant irascible character rather like Bernard Ingham. The interviewee was required to sit at a distant part of the room away from his desk which I thought rather odd so proceeded to pull the chair towards him. He exploded and told me to leave the chair where it was and not to rearrange the furniture. I learned later that he suffered from a condition which affected his eyesight and the distance was to keep the subject in focus.

He also said that he did not think it a required part of his job to help post-grads to find appoinments! However he would deign to see what he might do (in a minimum sort of way it seemed). This was the University appointments "Milk Round".

An appointment with the Canadian Atomic Energy Authority was one of the possibilities and a representative would be visiting Birmingham in the near future.

Also ICI did consider applications and he would pass my name to them.

The CAEA interview went quite well and was given by a recruiter from the British AEA on their behalf. I subsequently received an offer from CAEA but the level of remuneration ($6500) was not enough to induce me to make the move to Canada.

The ICI interview was fair and given by a pair of interviewers who were quite affable chaps and said they would pass my details on to the Dyestuffs division at Hexagon house Manchester. I later received an appointment to visit ICI pharmaceuticals at Grangemouth Stirlingshire. I visited there during the Easter vacation and was shown round the works which processed pharma chemicals on a batch process. I felt that the machinery and equipment was fairly simple and would be unlikely to provide much of a challenge or the opportunity to learn much about Mechanical Technology. However the interview proceeded and I had a chat with the site chief engineer which was pleasant enough. He then brought in a rather brusque (seemed to be in a hurry) English visitor to the plant who was based at Manchester and had an overarching position in the Dyestuffs Division. He asked me a few searching questions about the course which I did not answer well and he was in no doubt that I was not the material he wanted on board. I had the same opinion of the job. He expected me only

159

to seek expenses from Dundee rather than from Birmingham but I argued that postgrads did not enjoy the same holidays as undergrads. Anyway he bustled off and the congenial chief engineer happily agreed to my expenses claim.

After Easter back at Birmingham I concentrated on getting through the finals which meant deep study and long hours. Having cleared the finals I had another look for a position and applied to British Nylon Spinners and also to a Scottish Firm called British Hydrocarbon Chemicals (BHC) based at Grangemouth. I wrote to both and filled in their application forms.

BHC was owned jointly by BP and the Distillers Co. and their business was petrochemicals. My first response was from BHC's London office at Britannic house Green Park. I was invited for interview there and saw a nice English gentleman who ran a congenial interview. He seemed to be satisfied with me and said he would arrange an interview at Grangemouth when I would be able to see the plant. Their site was in Grangemouth and was the biggest complex there.

The complex included Ethylene plants (3), High density Polyethylene, Phenol/Cumene, Gasoline, Ethanol, Methanol, Butadiene, Hydrofluoric acid (a dreadful acid which was very aggressive requiring workers to wear 100% protective clothing) and Acrilonitrile (in construction). Naptha Feedstock came over the fence from the BP refinery and formed the raw material for all the processes. Large cooling towers dominated the site and it ran continuously 24/7, as they say now.

I was on holiday at Dundee on the date of interview and travelled by train via Edinburgh to Polmont station where the BHC car met me. I was interviewed by Mr Hooper the chief engineer. It was a good interview and I was impressed by the plant and equipment

160

which they had. There was a great deal of mechanical plant including gas engines and compressors. I went to lunch with the company secretary at the staff house which was a very nice large mansion in its own grounds. In the afternoon I was interviewed by Mr Carmichael, the deputy chief engineer.

I felt that BHC would be the best place to go if an offer was forthcoming.

On returning to Birmingham I worked with Les and Arthur on experiments with the exhaust gas muffler to determine coefficients of discharge under various conditions of gas flow.

The summer of 1964 was mainly pleasant and sometimes quite hot. There was an evening barbeque at Chad Hill and a social sit down after the eats.

With the experimental work complete I was able to tackle the writing up of the thesis and paid one of the departmental secretaries to type it up. It was then submitted to the library for binding and duly presented to the Department for assessment.

Senior members of the academic staff were sometimes in residence at Chad Hill temporarily. One evening after the coffee in the lounge I met the Professor of French, one Fraser McKenzie, who was known to play the harp and could be seen around Edgbaston pulling the instrument behind him on wheels.

I had meanwhile received an offer of employment at Grangemouth which I accepted and where I would start in September. At the same time, as often happens, I received another offer from British Nylon Spinners with whom I had had an interview earlier. This was a company based at Cwm Braan in Wales. I had to inform them that I had received an offer from BHC which I intended to accept.

161

So my time at Birmingham came to an end and I arranged to travel North to Scotland with Arthur Jamieson on completion of my residency at Chad hill. Arthur had joined us at Chad Hill when the lease on his house in Northfield came to an end and his wife and child went home to Arbroath. Later Arthur and I travelled north to our homes in his Jowett Javelin.

RCST George St. Glasgow (Strathclyde University)

At Weir Building RCST Montrose St. Glasgow

See image credits p267

163

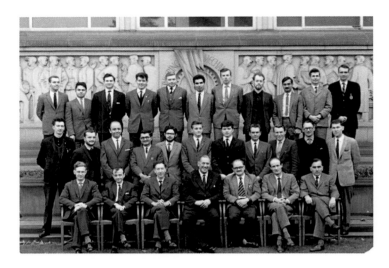

UoBirmingham 1963-4 MSc class Thermodynamics

Mechanical Engineering Building, University of Birmingham

164

Chad Hill residents 1963-4

Bill Fidler on back row with beard

Lab Project Trio Birmingham University 1964

165

Part 4 1964- 2004

British Hydrocarbon Chemicals

In August 1964 I arrived home to join Florence in preparing to move to Grangemouth. I had enquired of BHC regarding accommodation in Grangemouth and they said they would look into it. BHC and BP had their own housing there but also had pull in the Council housing department for key employees. I received a welcome call from BHC informing me that a house would be available with the local authority. This would be a 1960's flat of recent build and would be re-decorated prior to our entry.

I arrived to start at BHC one Sunday evening travelling by train to Grangemouth via Stirling and spent one night at the Park hotel prior to taking up residence at the BHC staff house. This was a modest mansion at the East end of Grangemouth and I was to report to a Mrs Saul, manager. Her frosty welcome suggested that I should have advised her of my arrival while I assumed that the BHC office had arranged all.

I spent my after-hours time of the first week visiting the allocated house and measuring up for curtains, getting together household cleaning stuff and a list of items I had not thought of. I ordered these from Urie the ironmonger on Grangemouth who was most helpful. The goods were provided and transported with me to the flat and the bill was presented at the end of the month. How civilised.

Back in Dundee Florence and I started to get together the essentials of setting up home which involved buying furniture, curtains, crockery etc etc. We engaged the Dundee Express Co to remove our stuff from Florence's parents' home and travelled with

167

the van to Grangemouth. Our flat was a relet at 28 Bankhill Court and was underfloor electrically heated and freshly repainted. My diary records that average weekly living expenses were £12 5s 7p (17 September 1964). We also bought a Perdio Caralux radio via BHC stores at a cost of £11 17s 4d and a wooden clothes airer from the Grangemouth Coop at 10 shillings (we are still using the latter in 2020). Shortly after taking up residence we noticed that the underfloor heating was not operating nor anything else electrical. I immediately went out to a local phone box and phoned the electricity people SSEB who came before long and replaced the main fuse which sorted the problem. I mentioned the fault to Mike Bennel the BHC Electrical Engineer and he was concerned enough to call his contacts at SSEB to investigate but the cause of the fuse failure was not discovered. Mike Bennell was decent chap and was sympathetic to the problems a young married couple would have in settling in to Grangemouth. He was in the process of buying a house in Dollar which was a popular place for BHC management to escape to after work in Grangemouth.

At the East end of Grangemouth, which was traditionally mainly a docks town, there was in that order the BP refinery and the BHC petrochemical works. BP was joint owner of BHC with the Distillers Co.

The BHC works straddled both sides of the Boness Road to the East of Grangemouth and comprised a large throbbing steaming fuming conglomerate of machinery houses, pipes. tanks, furnaces, cooling towers and few visible people. This was continuous process Petrochemicals manufacture with three shifts seven days per week 365 days of the year, intentionally anyway. A few blocks of 1940's brick built offices occupied the North frontage of the site facing the Road and these housed the senior management and engineering staff. There were also less permanent looking offices at other places within the works which were more closely associated with the plant daily operations and maintenance.

I reported to the company secretary and personnel officer Mr Finlay who directed me to the Training department where I was to undergo a three month period of orientation. Item one was that a hard hat and goggles were to be worn at all times. There were a trio of kindly gentlemen there who gave me an office based introduction to the main processes of the plants. As with most orientation courses this was intensive information bombardment which soon saturated the listener, but one got the general message. The general process in refining and petrochemicals was to heat up the feedstock to create vapour which was then condensed at a variety of temperatures producing different "fractions" of the hydrocarbon. In petrochemicals the difference was that chemical reactions were arranged to produce the useful product for example Ethylene. This Ethylene became an important building block of finished products such as polyethylene and many others. While in my first days there an excitement arose as a fire occurred, which I saw as a great smoking mass to the West, at the neighbouring BP refinery. I wondered at how calmly this was observed but I soon learned that plant upsets like this were to be experienced on a regular basis.

My training would take me to various plants within the BHC complex usually spending up to a week with the plant engineer of the respective plant.

The plant engineer's job was to manage the running maintenance of the plant by ordering work to be done on plant failures or pre-emptive maintenance.

I was asked by the training officer who I thought was the senior management person at BHC Grangemouth. Naturally I answered "The chief engineer, Mr Hooper" - wrong.

The senior manager was the General Manager of the site who was a chemical engineer. And so the penny started to drop, the big decisions would be made by chemical engineers and the "proper" engineers i.e. mechanical engineers would provide a service function i.e. maintenance. This was a function of the type of industry it was – chemicals production.

The second question was "what is the function of this company?" I ventured to say that it was the manufacture of petrochemical products – wrong. The function of the company was "to make money".

This had the secondary consequence that chemical engineers laid down the profit making designs to make the money and controlled the plant variables and mechanical engineers were a cost to keep the place running. This set the scene for a feeling of inferiority among the mechanical engineers. Also when plant failure occurred it was mechanical engineers who "felt the heat" to get things fixed.

There resulted two cultures within the complex, namely manufacturing operations (brown helmets) and manufacturing maintenance (black helmets). In addition to these divisions there were three smaller departments i.e. the Technical Services department, mainly chemical engineers, the Research Department, mainly chemists and the plant chemical laboratory. I was told that at craft level the engineering workmen were appropriate tradesmen while the operating department workers could be " ex butchers, bakers and candlestick-makers".

Support departments for plant maintenance were the engineering store and the engineering workshop.

My first assignment was visiting one of the chemical plants accompanying the plant engineer Bob Peatty on his daily round where he spoke to the engineering fitter foreman supervising work in hand. This could be on a failed pump or a leaking gland on a valve or replacing a gland seal on a shaft. Pumps etc. were often duplicated so that the process could continue while one pump was repaired on kept on standby.

I assisted on one problem by designing and drawing a pipe keeper assembly for workshop manufacture. The HF acid plant was one of his charges and he said not to go there unless really necessary and if it was required one had to don full protective clothing because of the aggressively corrosive chemical it was. It was said that the acid was so aggressive that a spot of it on the skin would eat its way in until it reached the bone.

On another of the plants highly concentrated sulphuric acid was pumped along stainless steel pipes. I asked if this caused severe corrosion of the pipes but learned that maximum corrosion was at 28% concentration in $H2O$.

Bob announced that it was time for a smoke and took me to a small isolated windowless wooden hut with hard seat benches inside. There were two other engineers there when we entered. This was a smoking hut as smoking was strictly prohibited on the plants or environs. Matches were also prohibited and the smoking hut was provided with a small low power electrical cigarette lighter. This was quite a social place and we had a chat with the others.

I had a regular weekly meeting with Mr Carmichael during this orientation period where we discussed what I had seen and he gave me guidance on the plants and future developments.

The next destination was the engineering Planning Department. This was located in a site office type of building among the plants to the south of BoNess Road. This building's ground floor was for operating staff lockers and a mess-room and the upper floor was offices for engineering managers and plant engineers. Manufacturing was split into product groups e.g. Olefins Group, Chemicals Group. Each group had a Group Chemical Engineer and a Group Mechanical Engineer. Below each of these were the plant chemical engineers and plant mechanical engineers. Operation of a plant was the responsibility of the plant chemical engineer. The plant mechanical engineer managed the maintenance of the plant. The plant was operated by "operators" and maintenance was carried out by engineering craftsmen - usually fitters but included plumbers, electricians, leadburners, welders and coppersmiths.

Supplying a general service to the site, as a separate service to maintenance, was the Instrumentation Department which supported the large amount of measuring equipment used in the processes. This was mainly pneumatic control as electrical devices were largely prohibited because of the fire and explosion risk prevalent everywhere on the plants.

The other general service department was electrical engineering with its own engineer and support staff and craftspeople.

This organization was necessary to run the 24/7 operation but in addition there were planned plant shutdowns to allow preventative maintenance to take place. These involved

172

overhauling and servicing of equipment to give high reliability operation.

This required detailed planning of work and ordering of spares and was the main function of the planning department. The chief planning engineer explained this to me and passed me over to his chief clerk for indoctrination. This included a required reading of the voluminous BHC standing orders. These were statements of company regulations or rules and were quite detailed and in great number. I ploughed through these and had to sign a paper after each volume that I had read them. The bald chief clerk was a studious looking middle aged gent and while he was a gentle type I did feel that I was being set up in some way. The chief planning engineer was ex airline engineering and he was a somewhat bitter about the way engineers were treated both in his previous job and here at BHC. He described engineers as "anybody's dogsbody". He was essentially saying that this applied to maintenance engineering in general.

The next group visited covered alcohols, acids and chemicals and the plant engineer was Bob Craig. I learned here that ethanol of purity greater than that used in whisky making was produced in a plant that had all its valves locked and under the control of HM Customs and Excise. Methanol was produced in the then newest plant which was the gas synthesis plant in the care of plant engineer Jerry Quayle. Here carbon dioxide and hydrogen were combined at high pressure to produce methanol. This required the mixture of gases to be compressed to 5000 pounds per square inch (psi) and exposed to a catalyst which produced methanol after condensation. The compressors were of the large reciprocating Cooper Bessemer gas engine driven type and the higher pressure was created using a reciprocating steam engine incorporating a massive flywheel. In order to contain the high pressure gas the pressure vessel was wound externally with high tensile steel wire, a method deriving from naval gun manufacture.

I then moved on to the plant engineering section whose job was to maintain common services of steam, water, building maintenance, pipelines and the finished product tankfarm. There were tankfarms at the BHC main site and at Grangemouth docks.

Included among the tanks were Hortonspheres i.e. the large spherical tanks for storing liquids under pressure which would otherwise boil and evaporate under atmospheric conditions. The plant engineer told of entering one of the sphere for maintenance purposes and seeing stuff like popcorn on the floor which had precipitated out of the contained product. If stood upon these popcorns would explode dramatically.

Other plants which were not visited included much the same type of plant and did not require to be included in my orientation tour. The exception was the Polyethylene plant which produced the high density type of polyethylene which withstood boiling water (HDPE). Prying eyes were not welcome in this plant as presumably the process had certain novel elements subject to high security.

My tour also included short visits to the main store and the plant accountant.

The main store manager, an Arts graduate, described how the value of spares held amounted to several millions pounds. The accountant said little about the performance of the company but implied that it did very nicely as the products selling price did not bear much relation to the manufacturing cost.

My diary records Pop songs at this time, November 1964, included the Beatles "Please Please Me" and "Let Me Hold Your Hand" with Adam Faith achieving a place in the top 10.

After several weeks on this tour I was assigned to a small section devoted to troubleshooting and special investigations. Ron Lyne was the engineer and I joined him in the south plant office mentioned earlier. It was an open style office with the senior managers located in individual offices on the periphery. There was a typing pool with a few young typists under the eye of Lena the senior typist. Mike Bennell the BHC Electrical engineer had an office as did Harold Sambrook Mechanical Maintenance Engineer. Group Engineer (Chemicals) had another office as did the Craft Engineer manager. In the body of the room were us engineers comprising plant Mechanical engineers, plant Chemical engineers, electrical engineers and the two safety engineers who tested work areas and issued gas free certificates if it was safe to do so.

My co-worker was Ron Lyne an Edinburgh University graduate who was a quiet contemplative type not given to outbursts or wasteful conversation. I was to work with him on plant problems requiring deeper investigation than the plant engineers were able to do in the hurly burly of everyday work. One problem Ron was dealing with was the failure of compressor valves. Compression of gases formed a large part of the BHC processes with compression followed by heating or cooling or treatment taking place in almost all the plants. This compression was, at my entry point, carried out by reciprocating compressors usually gas engine driven. The compressors used plate valves. The piston of the compressor compressed the gas and at some point in the stroke the outlet plate valve lifted and allowed the high pressure gas to pass from the cylinder to the next part of the process. There was a similar plate valve on the inlet (suction) valve.

The problem was that these valve plates failed by cracking and breaking up thus stopping the process on that compressor. The compressor involved would be taken out of service and the valve plate replaced. These failures were causing costly plant outages or flow reduction and the plates themselves were not cheap components. Ron's job was to record the statistics of valve plate failure and work towards more reliable plant operation. If there were 150 compressor cylinders with four valves per cylinder then at any one time 24 hrs per day 600 plate valves would be bouncing up and down against the cast iron valve seats. Progress was being made and Ron was introducing a more reliable valve plate made by Heidebegger of Austria. This was the stuff of troubleshooting. Another case he was on was the search for more effective sparking plugs on the methanol plant gas engines and he was testing aero engine type spark plugs there.

Note that these experiments had to be carried out on line on operating plant as there was no mechanical test lab as such. Thereby lay a problem because ideally an investigating engineer in testing a device has to measure variables and study the result of proposed changes. Therefore in the BHC case testing had to be carried out in-situ along with the effected changes occurring in plant operation. Clearly this was limiting as it was very difficult to isolate the effect of a change. Any instrumentation required for an investigation had to be non-electrical or gas safe which was a severe limitation on experimentation. There was also a cool reception from the chemical engineers to the carrying out of experiments by mechanical engineers. Any instrument used had to be intrinsically safe and the area of use had to have a gas free certificate which was entirely reasonable as major explosions could occur. Enough explosions occurred anyway without adding to them by introducing any more hazards.

The compressor valves job was Ron's baby and this suited me as it seemed a rather turgid ploy gathering up all the failure data and writing regular reports though it did have the merit of not requiring instrumentation for data.

In the midst of all this orientation Florence gave birth at Falkirk Royal Infirmary to Edward our first child. The BHC company sent her a bouquet to mark the event. This had been a difficult time for Florence in a strange town with few friends and few family visiting. I bought an old Humber Hawk car for £25 at this time and was able to drive mother and child home to 28 Bankhill Court Grangemouth. Though I say an old car it was only six years old but cars did not last long then.

I was alerted to a phenomenon on the Methanol plant Cooper Bessemer syn gas compressors. Syn (synthesis) gas was a mixture of hydrogen and carbon dioxide and was compressed to a few hundred pounds per square inch (psi) before going to the final 5000 psi compressor. The compressor was an integral construction i.e. the V8 gas engine driver and four cylinder compressor were in the same engine frame. The engine was turbocharged with an exhaust turbine. There were three of these compressors and one showed a lower turbo air pressure than the others. This pressure was measured in inches of water gauge using a U tube manometer (whoopee! an allowed measurement). I monitored this pressure over several weeks and it appeared to be a regular phenomenon. Having checked speed, spark plugs, intake arrangements, exhaust valve condition and found them the same there had to be something different.

The suspect compressor was due a minor service and I asked for the valve timing to be checked when it was off line. A compressor, where it was one of a group, could be shut down temporarily without shutting down the plant. This was done and the service carried out under the supervision of the capable foreman Jimmy Miller. It was found that the timing of the inlet valves was out by 14 degrees. This was met with some disbelief but it was checked and found to be so. The timing was adjusted and the compressor boxed up and put back on line. The result was not wholly a success with only a slight improvement in air pressure. However a point had been made re the accuracy of compressor valve timing.

One evening I was at home in Bankhill court kneeling on the carpeted underfloor heated floor when the ground rumbled and outside far off there was an almighty bang and several similar explosive sounds. I went out on to our balcony and looked east to the main plant area. The sky was illuminated in waves of light emanating in a spherical form from the plants. It was clear that a major failure had occurred however I took no action as the plant would be in the hands of the Company fire service and the local brigade also.

Next morning I learned that a major fire had occurred at the Methanol plant.

The high pressure syn-gas1 compressor, which was driven by a single cylinder piston steam engine, had a very large flywheel and the jam which had occurred had caused the flywheel to partially shear its key so there must have been a severe blockage somewhere on the fluid side. A failure had occurred which released syn-gas which immediately ignited and shot flame all round for probably 50 to 100 feet. There was a Bourdon pressure gauge, which I had often consulted, made of brass with a glass front. These gauges had a phosphor bronze bourdon tube which was the measuring element. After the incident I looked at the place where the gauge had been and only the Bourdon tube remained, the rest had been melted and vapourised. I do not remember a convincing reason being found for this system failure though much thought was applied to it. As I remember it the high pressure compressor cylinder showed considerable destruction. The main action was to get the plant back in action and this was done with great expedition and urgency. BHC staff were quite good at getting things back up and running after a destructive failure though in this case it would involve some major engineering refurbishment over a period of a few months.

About this time the process of achieving compression was going through change at the design level. There was a move to introduce rotary compressors of the centrifugal type and the first of these was seen in an extension to the capacity of the Propylene 3 plant. This plant had a set of Thomassen gas engine driven compressors and one new centrifugal compressor was added to the plant. There was some anxiety and nervousness about this innovation and the commissioning was going to be watched carefully. I had covered centrifugal compressors among others during my studies so the concept was not new to me. I had a look at the information available on the machine to be fitted to the propylene 3 plant and tried to find out as much as possible about it. It was to be electric motor driven and would be involved with the refrigeration duties in the plant process. I was asked to prepare operating instructions for the compressor and this I did with reference to the manual from the compressor manufacturer. The compressor was commissioned and seemed to run without any major problems. These plant extensions were usually carried out by oil sector contractors such as Stone and Webster, Kellog or

Fluor. I found that this arrangement made the construction and commissioning process rather opaque to the observer such as myself who was not directly involved. It was not easy to get to see, for example, drawings of the proposals.

When the plant was being brought up to operation after the shutdown for upgrade I was asked to take standby watches on the nightshift in case anything should go wrong.

The plant had run successfully on startup late afternoon and I turned up at 8pm and reported to the plant control room. The plant chemical engineer was there and we talked about the new compressor which seemed to be running ok. He decided to go home at 9 pm and left me with the plant operating foreman to keep watch. Things went ok till about 11pm when the temperature in the refrigeration section was noted to be falling progressively. There was nothing the plant foreman could do to correct this and he asked me for advice. I suggested we needed to call the plant chemical engineer who was preparing for bed but reluctantly said he would call in. He did call and after some analysis called for some of the reciprocating compressors to be shut down which brought things under control. I concluded that the chemical engineers had underestimated the capacity of the rotary compressor and it had been passing through too much refrigerant. The rest of the night went smoothly and I was able to proceed home after 7.00 in the morning. Next day there was something of a stir over the event and the management were pleased that I had acted to get the chemical engineer in.

However the downside was that the Olefins Group Mechanical Engineer insisted that I spend another night on standby just in case.

The new development at this time was the Acrilonitrile plant then being built by the Fluor Corporation to the East of the existing plants. I was assigned to take an interest in the rotary compressor plant on this and prepare the operating instructions for the Brown Boveri air compressor. This was a 3000HP compressor driven by the option of a steam turbine at one end or an electric motor at the other. I set about reading up the manuals for the machines in order to write up a series of instruction for startup. The plan was to start up with the steam turbine to reach synchronous speed i.e. the frequency of the mains and then switch in the motor at which point the steam drive was throttled down and ran idle. This was fine, the document was prepared, copied and distributed and I thought that I had done my bit until I received a call that I was to stand by on a night shift to run the compressor up.

Starting up a steam turbine has to be done with care and prior to opening the throttle there is a check list comprising steam drains, checking the lubricating oil system and steam supply. But the greatest of these is the steam drains. Steam is allowed to pass through at very low pressure to warm the turbine up and condensation then occurs which must drain off before rotation can start. So the drains had to be observed till clean steam issued from them free of water. The throttle was then slowly opened and the compressor started to rotate progressively but slowly till 3000 rpm was achieved.

I then had to press the rather surprisingly small start button for the 3000 horsepower motor and without a murmur drive passed to the motor and the steam turbine throttle could be closed.

The reason for this double drive was not entirely clear except that I knew that there must not be a loss of air pressure once the plant was running. Steam or electric drive could be chosen depending on availability of steam from the power station.

This plant had a 150ft tall vessel which looked like a large space rocket and at what would have been the pointed end was a stack pointing up to the sky. I was informed that if there was a plant upset compressed gas would be ejected high up into the atmosphere above the inversion layer and be carried away ... to where?

Hence the need for a dependable compressed air system. Years later I passed this plant on the Road and I could see that there had been obvious spillage of something on the outside of the "rocket" vessel. I should mention that this plant did use Hydrogen Cyanide as part of the process and if there was an upset this highly poisonous gas had to be dumped somewhere .. via the rocket stack??

After the compressor was successfully running I was able to leave the plant at about 6.00am. This was August and out of the sky there was dropping flakes of something. I asked but nobody there could say what it was. There were many times when I asked about an event that I got silence. There was a culture of cover up going on. Usually an unpleasant event was due to somebody's action and this had to be covered up. Especially the Operations staff did not wish to pass information across to the Engineering staff. So if one was investigating some plant anomaly it was sometimes difficult or impossible to find out what went wrong because of cover up.

Such were the things that happened and combined with the regular explosions and general bad smells I was going off the idea of staying in the Petrochem business.

I found out during my time in Grangemouth that almost all the engineers did not live in the town the favourite place being Edinburgh and a few in Dollar. It was beyond our resources to contemplate a move to either of these places so we felt a bit trapped in Grangemouth. There was something depressing about the flatness of the place and the limited facilities available that created a feeling of dissatisfaction.

My sister Edith and Her husband Gerald Strome were visiting Scotland in the summer of 1965 and they visited us in Grangemouth and we also visited them at their base in Dundee. Going back to Grangemouth after an enjoyable weekend in Dundee unsettled us somewhat and we began to think about alternative futures. Emigration to Canada was one of these and I began to look into that option. We got as far as setting a date to go and I submitted my notice to leave to BHC.

This caused major reaction from the General Manager at BHC and I was called to a meeting with him to explain my position. He asked me to attend another meeting at which the senior Engineering staff were present to try to seek a way forward which would keep me at Grangemouth. This did not produce any alternative which they or I was happy with.

We visited the Canadian Consulate in Glasgow on 19th August 1964 and had a medical from their doctor. The flights were booked with Air Canada out of Prestwick and we continued our correspondence with Edith setting up our move. However about this time my cousin Jim Donald's wife Helen was visiting Scotland from New Jersey USA and I met her in Dundee at my sister Ella's house. She wondered why we were planning to visit Canada which to her was a cold wilderness with much less opportunity than the USA. This encounter stopped me in my tracks and the

183

first seeds of doubt about the wisdom of going to Canada were sown. Also we were getting down to the nitty gritty of thinking about where we were going to live as we could not consider staying with Edie for more than a short time. So a gloom set in but was relieved by seeing an advertisement for Engineers at the National Engineering Laboratory (NEL) at East Kilbride.

The logical assessment went like this: I was not getting enough experience of a sound technological nature so - why was I planning to go to Canada where I was unlikely to encounter state of the art technology?. This led me to consider moving to a job where Mechanical Engineering Technology would be the main thing rather than a subsidiary activity as it was at BHC or any other process industry for that matter.

I had attended a pumps conference at NEL while at BHC and I was impressed by the work being done there and the general attitude to technological engineering.

I therefore applied to NEL and duly attended an interview on 30th August 1964 at which I must have satisfied them that I was suitable since an offer was received to the post of Scientific Officer (Temporary). The word temporary referred to the practice of entry officers being recruited to an unestablished position in the first instance and at a later point applying for establishment.

This was a great relief and we were able to see our way to progressing without the major shift to another country. In retrospect there would have been another way at BHC had it been acceptable to them. That would have been for me to continue to specialise in rotating machinery as that was to be a future major path of plant development. I would have wanted to visit the plant suppliers e.g. Brown Boveri, AEI, Sulzer and also study the design and operation to my and BHC's benefit.

184

However there was the point of accommodation quality and I would have wished to move to a house purchase situation with BHC's help. Perhaps all of this was too much to hope for. It certainly was not on the table at any of the meetings with management.

There was also the problem of Richard Lorge. He had been appointed as the Senior Mechanical Engineer over Ron and I. I imagine that he would not have been agreeable to me pursuing a path of career advancement which would mean me knowing more about the new machinery than he. He was also a difficult person to work under and was another nail in the coffin of my post at BHC.

The National Engineering Laboratory, East Kilbride

The date of my appointment at NEL in November 1965 approached and I had to work out how to get to East Kilbride on a daily basis until such time as we could move there. I had bought a six year old Humber Hawk car while in Grangemouth and this would allow me to get to Falkirk High station on the Edinburgh to Glasgow rail line.

Regular fast trains ran on this route into Queen Street station in Glasgow. A bus then took me 12 miles or so to East Kilbride. So this was to be a bit of a trail each day and back at night but there was little option other than me staying away during the week and home at weekends. I would rise at 5.45 each morning and be on my way to Falkirk High by 6.20 to catch a train about 6.50 arriving at NEL about 8.30.

The return trip got me home at about 7pm. This was a long day and I was not sure how long I would be able to keep it up. The Humber kept going through that winter with admirable reliability.

East Kilbride town was expanding at this time and houses were under construction.

I had made my need for accommodation clear to the NEL Personnel office and they were helpful in getting my name on the list for a Development Corporation house.

It was to be a seemingly long wait but by February 1966 I was notified that a flat would be available at 12 Thorndyke. This flat overlooked a valley of countryside in the near view stretching away to industrial Hamilton in the 15 mile distance. It was a good first floor flat, underfloor heating, brand new, with a living/dining area, hatch to the kitchen , two bedrooms, bathroom and a store room.

After my first daily long journey from Grangemouth I reported to the Machinery Group office at NEL where I was directed to the then new Naismith Building, Hydrodynamic bearings section.

The man in charge there was Bill Cook a forty something Senior Experimental Officer who originally hailed from Nottinghamshire. There were also two experimental officers and a technician. The section was housed in a bay of the building with a high roofed hall section and attached equipment/control rooms. The section had only recently moved into these new quite high quality premises from an outstation at Thorntonhall some eight miles or so towards Glasgow.

Bill was a medium height solidly built, but not stout, man who had been with the Lab since its inception in the 1940's. He had originally joined what was the NPL Lubrication section at Thorntonhall. He had a ruddy complexion and a somewhat hooked nose and was a stickler for detail in what he did and what he expected you to do. Bill had served in the Royal Navy in WW2 as a technical rating working on radio systems maintenance and on demob had studied for an HNC at a Technical College in Nottinghamshire his home county. On joining NPL as a Scientific Assistant he had developed an interest in electronic instrumentation and I was to have to shape up to his expectations in this field too.

The Hydrodynamic bearings section had been part of a much larger Division at Thorntonhall which involved wear, friction and lubricants for advanced machinery in support of Defence Departments and also British Rail. The leader of the Division had been Dr Fred Barwell who was a specialist in Rail to wheel interaction. Dr Barwell had gone on to become one of the first Professors of Tribology at Cardiff University.

Bill made it clear that I was expected to "fit in" whatever that meant. I was able to read up the respected texts on the subject which suited me fine; this was what I came to do. The work going on in the section included testing of high speed plain bearings under steady loading which was a long term project associated with the Admiralty Engineering division at Bath and also with a Bearing Design Methodology which was being developed by Dr Bob Woolacott at NEL.

Bill suggested that I should carry out further work on the electronically instrumented engine connecting rod he had designed and developed. There were in fact two rods: one for measuring displacement of the big end journal in its bearing and the other for measuring axial force in the rod both of these to be tested in an actual engine.

While these rods had been manufactured they had at this time not been tested.

It became evident that this was the field of Dynamically loaded bearings i.e. the load varied with direction and time continuously and is the type of bearing commonly used in all reciprocating piston engines.

I set about getting to know the instrumentation to be used which was in the main DC amplifiers made by Southern Instruments. This was the era of valve amplifiers and these were plagued by drift and low input impedance. What this meant was that a transducer output , e.g. a strain gauge, connected to the amplifier would change due to ambient temperature, a draught, or other changes in the amplifier while under steady load. So a calibration would be carried out and because of drift this calibration would be off during the experiment. In addition the Southern Instruments kit was getting quite old and unreliable and we regularly had to repair faults.

The low input impedance of these amplifiers was a problem because as the transducer changed its physical quantity e.g. resistance this had an effect on the gain of the amplifier and therefore gave a false result. I was to spend a lot of time just struggling to keep this instrumentation working long enough to get some measurements made.

A way round the problem was found by using a cathode ray oscilloscope or "scope" which had high input impedance. Also transistor based amplifiers were becoming available which had a high input impedance and reliability.

I learned that before any data could be gathered that the equipment had to be calibrated where possible under conditions of temperature to be experienced.

This involved designing a metal box for the connecting rod heated by a hot air gun and the assembly mounted in a tensile testing machine.

The work progressed and a set of operating data were collected with the force measuring rod used in a single cylinder Petter Diesel engine. The rod had a strain gauge which detected the force in the rod and the resulting signal was transmitted by radio to a stationary aerial in the engine crankcase i.e. telemetry. The tests were run and graphs of force on a base of time were recorded using a galvanometer type device which exposed a photographic paper strip. This was then exposed and developed to provide the desired results.

When it came to the displacement measuring rod everything was set for an experimental run and the engine was started but came to halt after a short time. It was found that the big end bearing had failed and there was evidence of melted white metal. The technician assembling the engine had omitted a critical part which meant the oil supply to the bearing was cut off. This was another most frustrating event in a long series of equipment failures and Bill decided to close off the work and concentrate on other more topical projects.

We were settling in at East Kilbride and had a weekend break in April at Kenmore caravan park where there was a family gathering. Robbie and family, Ella and family and my parents with each family in its own caravan. This was an enjoyable weekend in somewhat cool weather but our Bluebird caravan did have a coal fire which warmed us up. The weekend was also slightly unsettling as I felt the lack of family contact with living away from Dundee.

Later in mid August 1966 we had two weeks holiday. We did not go away to a resort but had a trip to Dundee for a few days and also from East Kilbride Florence and I and Edward took the bus into Glasgow to board the Queen Mary II for a trip "Doon the watter". This was a fine days outing with a squeeze box trio playing on board. We disembarked at Gourock and took another boat across to Dunoon, where we saw the nearby US Navy ships in the Holy Loch, returning to Gourock and then by train back to Glasgow.

In September 1966 I joined a group from our lab and flew to Nottingham to attend the IMechE Lubrication of reciprocating engines conference. This was my first experience of flying. We travelled to Abbotsinch airport (now Glasgow Airport) and boarded a Handley Page Dart Herald turboprop for a noisy slightly bumpy flight to East Midlands airport. The event was at Nottingham University and I was impressed by the quality of the residence accommodation set in a lovely park campus. Professor Harry McCallion's department hosted the event and there were quite a group of speakers from among his colleagues which were mainly research students. The use of computers featured strongly in the presentations and reflected the trends of the time.

It was a good experience and I enjoyed the technical atmosphere of it and seeing the international big names in Friction, Lubrication and Wear soon to be called "Tribology".

In November 1966 our section was invited to contribute to the "Engineer's Day" exhibition at the Science Museum, South Kensington, London. A single cylinder engine was despatched to London by NEL van and I followed with a technician, Bert Fraser, by sleeper the following week. We saw to the installation of the engine and the stall allocated to NEL. The object of the exhibition

190

was to promote engineering as a career to young people. The Queen was to open the exhibition in due course. I declined the invitation to be there for the Queen's visit and Bill Cooke attended. I had had enough of travelling to London and living in B&Bs on 30 shillings per night accommodation.

About this time I decided to apply for establishment. This was a process of becoming an established Civil Servant and required the candidate to sit an interview or "Board" at the Civil Service Personnel Department in Saville Row London. Here I made a mistake. I was in the middle of attending a course in Sheffield and I did not avail myself of a practice interview at NEL which would have prepared me for the Board.

The Board was to take place on a Monday morning and I arranged to fit it into my returning to Sheffield after a weekend at home in East Kilbride. This meant travelling by sleeper to London which I did and arrived in pouring rain. I put in some time at the National Gallery till my appointment and then made my dripping way to the austere Saville Row office.

This was my first experience of the grilling interview situation in which the candidate is faced by the interview team of three or four interrogators. I suspect that my attitude was perhaps a bit casual and also my answers could have been better with some coaching and preparation. The result learned a few weeks later was that I had failed to pass the board. This was somewhat destabilising and Made me wonder about my future at NEL. Of course I would be able to sit another Board after a time but I did feel peeved.

The next project was the design of a dynamically loaded bearing rig (DLBR). This rig was to simulate the forces acting on a bearing subject to dynamic loads as in an engine.

The load was to be generated by hydraulic rams controlled electronically using "Moog" valves. This was a major rig and had been in progress for some time.

I was assigned the task of designing a method of varying the speed of the shaft i.e. crankpin such as to simulate the varying speed as in an engine due to con rod obliquity.

The speed of the crankpin in a big end bearing relative to the bearing does vary as the crankshaft rotates. This is due to the con rod "swinging" as the piston goes up and down. It was required to simulate this motion in the DLBR. One solution would be to drive the DLBR shaft (ie crankpin) at a speed which varied during one revolution i.e. cyclically varying rotational velocity. Bill and I brainstormed this problem and of several options the chosen method involved using a universal joint to drive the shaft.

A universal joint has a varying output velocity for a steady input velocity and I found that the required amount of variation could be achieved by having two such joints in series. The other problem was to prove that the required variation was indeed being achieved. This latter requirement was met by attaching a diffraction grating to the shaft and measuring the velocity change via an optical pickup. This latter I had to design as there was none available at the time. The resulting set up can be seen in the photographs section.

About this time Bill was to have some leave and he warned me that there would be a visit of important industry people and that I would have to handle the visit to our section. The visitors turned out to be Alec Issigonis of BMC and Mr Heynes of Jaguar. This was a rather daunting prospect but was a wonderful opportunity to meet these distinguished people. Issigonis had famously designed the Morris Minor and the Mini while Heynes was Jaguar's chief engineer and leading engine designer.

The visit was rather stilted I thought but I went ahead and described the work we were doing especially the dynamically loaded bearing rig. Heynes did not say much but Issigonis was relaxed and gentlemanly and made encouraging remarks and then they were gone to the next department.

This was all good stuff and I was achieving my intended result which was to learn more detailed technology in the Tribology area. To this end I had attended a Tribology course at Sheffield University at which I learned much more about the wider Tribology field including wear and friction, lubricants and rolling element bearings. However things were getting a bit strained and claustrophobic plus disagreements were beginning to happen between Bill and I.

This came to head when I wrote up the variable speed work in an NEL report and wrote the authors as myself and Bill. He took exception to this order and we had a bit of a discussion over it. He chose to raise this in the presence of a junior member of the team which I felt was not good form and though I offered to change the order of names on the report he was by that time in a fit of pique. This was just the catalyst for change as promotion prospects were not good anyway and there were no other sections at NEL which I wished to transfer to. I therefore started to look elsewhere for opportunities.

I answered an advertisement for a Mechanical Engineering lecturer at Dundee College of Technology and attended for interview one October day in 1967. The head of Department was Dr John Kerr a Northern Irishman of open nature and pleasant but firm manner. I was shown round the Department with another candidate and this was followed by lunch at the Royal Hotel Union Street and a one to one interview in the afternoon. I was seen second and had time to visit Bill Fidler who was a serving lecturer at the College.

The interview went well enough and Dr Kerr said that a flat would be available on a fixed term basis to allow the new lecturer to settle in. I had many questions for Dr Kerr and time was running out before his next appointment so he invited me to his home in Glamis Drive on the next day, Saturday, to continue the discussion. I came away from the interview feeling that I could do the job justice but I was not impressed by the accommodation for the teaching staff and a general impression of lack of funding in the Institution at large. At that time the College was offering degree level courses awarded by the Council for Academic Awards (CNAA) and I gathered that there was a continuous struggle to sustain that accreditation level with mounds of paperwork to complete regularly. I did receive an offer of the position but decided that I could do better. In later months I was to regret that decision but ploughed on till something turned up.

In February 1968 Florence gave birth to our daughter Fiona at Hairmyres hospital. Florence's mother Mary came from Dundee to assist at our flat while Florence was in Hospital. We had no car at this time and I went with 3 year old Edward to collect Florence and Fiona and took a taxi home.

I applied to Rolls Royce at Hamilton and to SSEB (South of Scotland Electricity Board) at Cathcart Glasgow. These were both Mechanical Engineering technology positions with higher pay and a more applications environment.

I attended an interview at Rolls Royce and got a flavour of the work there. I had an offer from them and was given time to consider this. It did seem to require a lot of paperwork to get anything done. I had an offer of an interview from SSEB and was considering this when I spotted an Ad for University of Dundee looking for a lecturer in Mechanical Engineering.

I applied to the University having checked that accommodation might be available and in due course received an invitation to attend for interview.

I turned up for interview on a glorious spring day at the new University of Dundee in April 1968. The University had been Queens College Dundee till June 1967 but had been a University College since 1882. As I stepped into the Tower building foyer there was an immediate impression of quality and substance. The porters on duty were in smart uniform and guided me to the interview place on the fourth floor. The interviews were to take place in the Baxter Room which was a panelled room resplendent with oil paintings, plush carpet and quality board room type furniture.

There were four of us candidates and we were placed in a waiting room which was in fact the office of the deputy secretary complete with ample seating and a few national daily newspapers. The interview secretary notified us that we would be seen in alphabetical order.

When my turn came I was conducted to the Baxter Room to find a group of people sat round the large table. The chairman was Professor Dick of Mechanical Engineering, supported by Professor Culwick, Dean of Engineering and Applied Science and Professor of Electrical Engineering, Professor of Civil Engineering Tony Cusens. Ross Williamson Senior Lecturer in Mechanical Engineering and Jim Robertson of the Law Department he satisfying the requirement for an academic from out-with the faculty. This was a seemingly high powered interview panel and might have been intimidating had I not had experience of a similar gauntlet in the Civil service.

I fielded the questions from the panel members as best I could. It helped that Prof Dick had a background in Lubrication and I was able to weave into my answer the trouble that the local power station was having with their turbo alternator bearings.

The Dean was suitably satisfied that I had been using electronic instrumentation and Prof Cusens asked something about telemetry. Ross Williamson asked me if I would be willing and able to do the academic part of the job. I did not have an answer for this but was able to say that I had coached some apprentices in engineering science while at BHC and had enjoyed the experience. I was asked if I had any questions for the panel and I had to say I would like to know what salary would attach to the post.

I was told that it would be the first point on the lecturer scale. I said that I had hoped for more as I had a few years' experience. I also said that I had hopes of buying a house and that the offered level of salary would not allow this. I was told that it was teaching experience that mattered not research or industrial experience. This would prove to be an inaccurate statement. I left the room after the interview and was asked to sit outside.

I could hear them discussing the case including someone saying "This is the problem" and eventually the interview secretary came out and said that I would hear from the University in due course and that if I wished I could speak to the University property manager about available accommodation. I trust that the salary level expected was "the problem"

I did approach the Works department office and spoke to a Mr Miller who was able to say what accommodation may be available but that it would depend on what was available at the time of taking up post.

A few days later an envelope did arrive in the mail at 12 Thorndyke, East Kilbride with an offer of appointment as Lecturer in Mechanical Engineering. The offer included one point up on the Lecturer scale at £1560 per annum but I was disappointed that it was not more. Florence and I discussed the letter and I was of the opinion that it was not on but Florence felt strongly that it would be good to get back to Dundee. This surprised me but then I did not have the same need for friends and relations that she did.

However I was glad to agree to accept the offer and answered accordingly.

I gave my notice in writing to the Director of NEL, by that time Mr David Penny, that I was to leave on Friday the 17th June 1968. I worked out my notice clearing things up and handing back books from the NEL library. I left at lunchtime on the last day with a half days leave to take and Bill walked with me up the Road from the Lab.

Overall NEL had been a good experience and I felt that I had achieved my aim.

East Kilbride had been a good place to live though lacking the established recreational and cultural things one finds in older towns e.g. parks, museums and libraries.

I discovered when I took up my position at Dundee University that I had made a mistake in finishing on a Friday and starting the new job on a Monday i.e. nobody pays for the weekend.

Dundee University

We engaged the Dundee Express Co. To move our household belongings from East Kilbride to 19 Airlie Place Dundee. Edward was 3 and Fiona 4 months. When the van was loaded and set off we travelled by taxi to Buchanan St Rail station in Glasgow to board the Dundee train. It was a good feeling to be returning to our home town. There were Glasgow mothers and children boarding the train and they looked like they were going to Angus for the berry season. As we approached Dundee I noted that rail workers were lifting the branch line to Lochee and Blairgowrie.

My sister Rena had kindly been getting 19 Airlie Place in order for us to move in which had involved getting electricity and water etc arranged and cleaning up after the previous occupants. The flat was on the ground floor right and comprised two bedrooms, living room and kitchen with a bathroom off the kitchen and a WC off the hall. It had been built in the late 19th century. Heating was by coal fire. Airlie Place was a cul de sac with terraced villas on each side leading up to a Victorian grassed square flanked by tenements and along the top by another tenement known as Airlie Terrace. The student residence Airlie Hall occupied the left side going up and the Terrace and the right side including No 19 was occupied by University staff.

I reported on Monday 17th June at the Mechanical Engineering Department in the University's Fulton Building in Small's Lane. The building dated from 1963 and was the new home of the Departments of Mechanical Engineering and of Civil Engineering. A second development of the building was nearing completion and I would ultimately have one of the new offices looking to the South towards the river.

I met Professor of Mechanical Engineering John Dick who had been at Dundee since 1954. He said they were about to have their examiners meeting so I would be free to get settled in the flat and he would see me the next day.

I returned next day and had an introductory talk with Professor Dick. He told me where to go to formally state my presence and start date to the University Finance Officer. I was given a temporary place to sit in one of the lecture rooms No H2.

Since this was the end of the summer term there would be no lectures or tutorial duties to do but the Professor outlined what I would be doing in October when the new session started. This would be to support tutorial classes in second year Dynamics, second year thermodynamics, first year Engineering Drawing and first year principles of Engineering. Meanwhile I was given the task of producing solutions to a new set of Principles of Engineering tutorial examples which he had prepared. This was an exercise and perhaps a test of my ability also. These were examples in the area of basic applied mechanics and I suspect that they were of the type John Dick had used when he was at Oxford University prior to taking up the appointment at Queens College, St Andrews University in 1954.

I worked away at these examples with some reference to books on the subject. Some staff in the Department would look in from time to time to introduce themselves.

The first member of staff to visit was Ben Robb who was the senior Scientific Officer for the Department. Ben was a Higher National man who had served an apprenticeship in Blackness Foundry Dundee which was a manufacturer of textile machinery mainly but had branched out into machine tools when the textile business declined. He had then worked in Babcock Cranes design office in

Dundee, Astral Refrigerator Co and NCR Development department before joining University of Dundee. He was to give the first year drawing lectures which I would assist with as part of my assignment. Ben was an able colleague who assisted me greatly to settle in to the Department and it was a great and tragic loss when he succumbed to cancer at age 47.

Next to visit was John Fleming a Glaswegian lecturer who was about to leave the Department for Strathclyde University. John rolled his own cigarettes and would punctuate his animated discussion with quick licks of the cigarette paper before lighting up the inflammable assembly. He was a Strathclyde graduate who had worked for a consulting engineering company which had designed the heating and ventilating systems for the Fort William pulp mill. He had not been in Dundee long and was returning to his home turf.

Ross Williamson, one of the two senior lecturers in the Department, looked in. Ross had been on my appointment board so I had already met him over the "grill room" table.

He was a decent man who had been in the Department for some years, probably since the 1950's. Originally from Scotland and a graduate of University of London he had had appointments at the Fuel Research station and Woolwich College of Technology before joining Queens College. Ross was the senior Thermodynamics lecturer taking the third and fourth (Honours) year classes. Ross bought a new car each summer and travelled to Spain for the summer holiday. His wife Betty was a teacher of Spanish at Dundee High School.

I was trying by this time to work out who my next senior officer was and Ross told me that it was the Head of Department Prof Dick.

Peter Bissell, a Black country Brummy, was another of the lecturers who looked in. Peter was a Sheffield graduate and I was never sure what he had done since graduation but it did seem to include some vacation work in Sweden and a University appointment in Nigeria. Peter was an active type, full of energy and had to be *doing*. He was a restless sort of chap and whatever he did had to be done quickly it seemed. He lectured the second year Design course. Peter introduced the teaching of Manufacturing Engineering within the Department which was a useful and timely addition as far as I was concerned. It was an uncomfortable addition for some staff however.

Peter was liable to take unpaid leave to work in foreign countries such as Nigeria and the Manufacturing courses would ultimately be given by Ben Robb and I.

Hector Hetherington was a quiet enigmatic gentleman from Lockerbie and of the old school. Hector would be about 5ft 2ins and wore tweed suits. Little was said beyond a clearing of the throat. I was to learn later that he suffered from a diabetes condition which may have explained his reserved demeanour.

John Spence looked in. John was a friendly normal sort of person who had been raised in Hackney London and had been an undergraduate at Queens College Dundee of the University of St Andrews in the early 1950's. He had worked after graduation at Ferranti Edinburgh and then at Hatfield Polytechnic before joining the staff at Dundee. He lectured to the second year Dynamics class and assisted at tutorials in other courses.

There were a few others whom I would have to go and seek.

Professor Dick talked at me and suggested that I could assist James Baxter-Brown in supervising a particular Honours student. I thought that having two supervisors for one student a bit odd but anyway I went along to visit Jim in his room and from the start felt that I was intruding. I tried to find out what research he was doing and did little but scrape lightly at the surface of knowledge of his activities. I then told him that Professor Dick suggested that I assist in supervising a particular Honours student namely IA. This took him by surprise but he did say that if I wanted I should take over the supervision. This suited me better as I could not see how two supervisors-one student would work. Jim was a bit of a loner and I did not trouble him much again.

The immediate future teaching task was thus taking shape but at this time did not include any actual lecturing. This seemed to be Professor Dick's way and I did not seek to change it.

I did want to know what research was going on in the Department and set about trying to determine this by asking people face-on what research they were doing. Mistake.

I approached Ian Davidson and David Watt a pair of lecturers that worked closely together. Ian Davidson lectured in Fluid Mechanics and David Watt in Dynamics. On asking about their research work I got a rather negative response.

The remaining member of staff was Archibald Hall who had been in the Department the longest time and probably pre WW2. Arch was a rather bluff and blustery Dundonian who had served an apprenticeship at the Caledon Shipyard's Lilybank Foundry Dundee in the 1920's. From there he had gone to sea as a marine engineer. The story goes that his father, also a marine engineer, visited his son in a ships engine room and instructed him in no uncertain terms to become an engineering student at the then University College Dundee. This would be in the 1930's when jobs were getting very scarce. He did graduate and stayed on to study for a PhD and joined the staff as a junior lecturer. I did not find him approachable and kept my distance.

Finally I cornered Ian Fitzpatrick another of the younger group; a West-Midlander from West Bromwich and a Materials Scientist. This was a newish subject category which encompassed the study of modern engineering materials including mainly metals and plastics but other materials were beginning to feature such as ceramics and fibres. Ian came from family background of metalworking business people and spring making had been their speciality. He had studied at UMIST Manchester and had gained a PhD there before joining the staff at Dundee. There had been the intention by the Faculty of Applied Science that Ian would service both the Departments of Mechanical and Civil Engineering. As it transpired Professor Dick had presumably made a strong case for Ian to be in Mechanical engineering. The same had been intended for Ben Robb. There was therefore a recent past history of division between these Departments and ne'er the twain would meet unless at faculty board meetings.

The structure of the Mechanical Departmental staff was becoming clear and comprised two main bodies of cohering people i.e., roughly, the younger and the older.

The Departmental secretary was the formidable Mrs Jack. Younger members of staff were below her field of vision but had to be officially tolerated it seemed. She ran a tea club in a windowless room which the older members attended. I kept my distance from this as I had learned in other places that tea clubs were often a source of disagreement and vituperative argument. The neighbouring Department in the Fulton Building was Civil Engineering and they ran a tea club in the new purpose built staff common room. The younger ME staff members gravitated to this club so I joined them there.

Other members in the Department were Derwent Turnbull, who was appointed at the same interview panel as me but took up his appointment some months later, and Oliver Roberts. Both were ex Royal Navy instructor officers and their contribution would be mainly in teaching. Derwent was an accomplished oboist and was the University Music co-ordinator.

From my survey of what research was being pursued I got a general impression from staff that there was so much teaching to do that there was little time for research.

I raised the question of what research to do with Professor Dick and he advised me to do work which would result in learned paper publication.

I gave this some thought and decided that I would do some work on the wear of steel in lubricated conditions. This arose from an industrial enquiry related to pressed parts being made by the NCR company in Dundee. They had been approached by a Swedish steel maker who claimed that they had a kind of steel to sell, "Hardflex", which edge hardened when sheared as in the pressing operation.

To prove this I proposed setting up a rig with samples of Hardflex and standard steel normally used in presswork. A benefit of this material, if it worked as claimed, was that an edge hardening operation was avoided.

My experience with the complexity of rigs for bearing work taught me to aim for some experimental work with simple instrumentation and drives.

I designed a wear machine comprising a rotating shaft against which test samples could be pressed to simulate a sliding wear situation. This rubbing contact was lubricated by a drip feed device which dropped liquid paraffin to maintain a wet contact. The machine could also be used to test dry rubbing contact e.g. plastic to steel which was an established bearing pair gaining currency in light engineering designs.

Two machines were manufactured and provided many students with Honours year projects. The lubricated wear result showed that in adhesive wear the Hardflex did provide enhanced wear life. Other materials tested included PTFE and also our own lab-produced carbon fibre reinforced white metal.

I attended lectures and visits of the British Association for the advancement of Science annual meeting which was held in Dundee in the summer of 1968.

In preparation for the start of session in October 1968 I was working on many of the tutorial problems which students would be tackling. This was a good education in itself including many Oxford sourced Mechanics questions produced by Professor Dick for the first year Principles of Engineering course..

Another challenge was first year Engineering Drawing. I had of course done much drawing but had never seen anything like the analytic drawing taught at Dundee University. Much of it, I later discovered, was Mongian geometry and comprised graphical methods of solving problems in Mechanics. It was quite ingenious stuff and in the days before general use of computers served a useful purpose. Examples I remember included the stability of an earth dam and also bending moment and shear force diagrams for beams. There was little emphasis on machine drawing which I felt would have been more relevant. This would follow in second year Design.

I also assisted in second year Dynamics tutorials for which the lectures were given by John Spence. The tutorial questions were tough but quite educational.

I was seeing a more analytic approach to Engineering Education than I had experienced at Dundee Technical College or Strathclyde University.

Florence and I were settled in to the flat at 19 Airlie Place and she was making friends with other academic wives. The flat was typical of the "rather better but not great" Victorian flat with an inside toilet and a bathroom in a built on tower to the rear clearly an addition to the original building. The heating for the flat was one coal fire in the sitting room and nothing else but we did have our portable electric fire which helped. With the winter in prospect our minds turned to buying a house with adequate heating. There were other problems at Airlie place a principal one being that it was in a student accommodation area and there were noisy nights to endure sometimes particularly if there was some sort of jape on. The student "Dines" was a recent building at the back of our flat rear garden area and the Saturday evening student hops there were quite loud. We were also finding a lack of open space in the area to exercise our two children.

The University Finance Officer told me that there was an arrangement with the Halifax Building Society whereby members of staff were given a guarantee by the University which allowed the Society to offer a higher %ge loan usually 95%. At that time the Halifax Building Society was a sober Yorkshire based organisation whose main business was supporting house purchasers rather than its present form which appears to be that of a commercial bank. There were a limited amount of funds on offer but I was given to understand that there should not be a problem and that I should seek the advice of a solicitor preferably other than the Macdonald practice which was getting a large slice of the University staff mortgage business. I therefore looked in on the Fergusson Stephen and Norrie practice inn Castle Street and declared my interest. Mr Norrie was a very pleasant person and he advised me to look at the Courier property ads for something within my purchasing limit. This was limited to three times my salary which at the time was £1560 per year.

We looked at several properties which one of us liked but not the other. The sensible thing to have done would have been to buy in East Balgillo which was then being built by Bett Bros. The consensus of choice of area lay in the Broughty Ferry area where there appeared to be good park space and shopping. There was a good bungalow in Nesbit Street which was ideal but needed work done and there was no budget for that as the deposit would use up all of our savings. Another was a Leven in the Dawson Park estate but the accommodation was too small for our needs.

Having spent some time looking round one would not think that we would end up buying a dog of a property. However Claypotts Castle Gardens did tick many of our immediate need boxes. Three bedrooms, generous lounge dining room with hatch to kitchen, attractive outlook on to Claypotts Castle, cul de sac, small garden and most important: gas warm air central heating.

We made an offer within our means and in November of 1968 we were moved by Dundee Express to our new home. When it came to paying the bill I noticed that we were being asked to pay for the wooden shed in the rear garden which had not been mentioned before. I thought this mean of the seller and I refused to pay and never did.

The gas warm air heating did "work" but I did not like the on-off temperature control which meant a sudden drop in temperature when the thermostat shut of the warm air supply. There was not the heat capacity which is a feature of hot water radiators and which gives a more even temperature with time. There was also a coal fireplace which did help in the coldest weather. As a space for living it was quite good but the poor quality of build would become evident. This was noticed first when the paint on some outer plywood panels began to blister. Repainting did not cure the problem which turned out to be due to moisture vapour passing through the panel to then condense under the gloss paint finish. A vapour barrier would have cured this and should have been included by the Builder Docherty.

I also noticed that there was, in cold weather, a lot of condensation on the large sitting room windows. Okay, they were single glazed but I suspected there was another reason and I suspected that there was leakage of the burnt gas into the warm air intake. This may also explain the dry slightly smoky smell. I read up on the matter and found that the short gas exhaust pipe with "ventile" outlet on the side of the house was not working well. In even a slight wind the rising air pressure between our house and the neighbouring house would cause the gas exhaust to feed back in to the cupboard in which the heating appliance was located. This was also the place where the warm air intake was located and therefore combustion products were being blown into the living spaces of the house. I designed an exhaust pipe which took the exhaust above the level of the roof of the house with an approved gas board terminal.

This solved the problem and the windows were noticeably drier and the air fresher.

However this was only one of the problems and the next one was not to be simple to fix. One summer's day I noticed a distinct unpleasant smell at the back door. On inspection I saw the level of fluid at a drain cover was visible. This suggested that there was a back up in the sewage system. As the examination proceeded I learned that our row of houses shared a common collector drain and we were near the low end of it. So if someone higher up the system put a blockage item in the toilet it could choke at the lower corner of the run of pipe and back up. This meant that those, like us, had to pay for the plumber to clear the blockage. Ideally each house should have an individual soil drain to the main Street sewer. So yet another snag with the house design was uncovered but with no practicable remedy.

I was successful in getting the Department to fund my visit to the IMechE Tribology (ie Friction lubrication and wear) conference in Gothenburg Sweden in September 1968. This was my first international conference and indeed my first visit outside the UK.

It was an agreeable experience and gave me an insight to another society. The impression was of a clean-cut prosperous country with leanings to Germany rather than the UK. One of the visits was to the Gothenburg Shipbuilding yard where I noted the youthfulness of the management team.

With time my salary increased and I was keen to move house if the opportunity arose.

We heard of a traditional bungalow, coming up for sale. I had by this time learned my lesson about modern house design and the corners that builders would cut and I had identified a detached brick built house with pitched roof to be the ideal.

We looked at the bungalow and I liked it immediately. Florence had to think about it but I convinced her that staying at the house at Claypotts was unsustainable in my mind. After some examination and valuation our offer was accepted and we moved by Dundee Express in April 1971. I had feared the Claypotts house would be hard to sell but we did not pitch the price too high and it went fairly quickly. Not much profit but a load off my mind. These flat roofed houses have since had pitched roofs fitted and in my opinion are improved.

At the Department of Mechanical Engineering I was trying to get a lecture course of my own to deliver. At this time, 1969, most of the courses were allocated to staff and there appeared to be a good staff to student ratio. These were soon to be looked upon as halcyon times as budgets and staff replacements were put under pressure.

I made it known that I would like to teach a Thermodynamics course and second year Thermo was coming up for review so I made a bid for that course at the staff meeting at which the next session's courses were discussed. I was not given much encouragement from the established staff who were a conservative lot. However I sustained my case and I was allocated second year Thermodynamics (Thermo).

I read up the specification of the second year Thermo course and set about reading up the content referring to the recommended text by Spalding and Cole.

Mechanical Engineering degree programmes typically comprised a set of courses including Thermodynamics, (Engineering)

Dynamics, Fluid Mechanics, Solid Mechanics (aka Strength of Materials), Engineering Design. Mathematics with other subjects such as Materials Science, Metrology and Manufacturing in addition. Universities would place different emphasis on composition of the programme depending on their tradition or latest trends as they saw them. The newer staff in 1968 were trying to include Manufacturing into the degree programme and we were having some limited success. There was no tradition of Manufacturing and difficulties were experienced. Dundee had a particular leaning to Mathematics but given by the Maths Department. Other Institutions, e.g. Strathclyde, would deliver the Mathematics course from within the Engineering Department and usually the latter model was better received by the staff and students in those places. My own view was that there appeared to be at Dundee University an emphasis on Mathematical proofs rather than on applications the latter being more relevant to Engineering.

Anyway at the time I had to accept things as they were and get on with the job.

Thermodynamics as a course was usually well received by the students. It had an obvious relevance to Engineering practice and had as a main objective the optimisation of heat engines systems' energy consumption.

Dundee University had had in 1963 a significant upgrade of its Mechanical Engineering laboratories and staff accommodation as could be seen in the Fulton Building which was shared with Civil Engineering.

My second year task was to deliver a one hour lecture once per week backed up by tutorial (i.e. examples) classes and laboratory sessions (labs). The labs would include trials of a diesel engine and also of a compound reciprocating steam engine.

There were two end of term class examinations and a degree exam in May to be set and also a degree exam resit in September. Department staff were expected to help with their colleagues' lab sessions and tutorial classes.

In the fourth, aka Honours, year students chose three major courses from the standard set, and also a specialist course from a list which reflected staff experience.

I offered Tribology as my specialist course and this was resisted by the staff but did get adopted anyway because the Professor thought that it should be included.

Therefore my workload comprised: assisting with First year Engineering drawing, and also First year principles of Engineering, Second year Thermodynamics course , tutorials and labs, Second year Dynamics tutorials, Second year Design tutorials.

Class sizes were large in First year, usually about 60 or so as Civil and Electrical students were included usually but reducing to 20 or so Mechanical Engineering students in second year.

The Fulton building second development was completed as I arrived and I soon had an office to myself with a view over the University buildings to the River. The centrally heated office was fitted with fixed furniture of a bookcase, side table with drawing drawers with a carpet and a filing cabinet in addition. These were excellent working conditions.

What I did not realise at the time was that this was the end of a period of good funding for University accommodation and staff.

Economies and financial stringency would become the order of the day as we entered the 1970's.

The students we were getting at Dundee were in the main a good bunch of young people. There was a significant number of English based students and a few foreign nationals. Dundee was favoured by English applicants who had not achieved the "A" levels required for English Universities. It should be noted that the Scottish Honours Degree programme was of four years duration whilst the English one was three years.

The English students' A levels reached a higher level over a narrower syllabus. The number of years of study from the start of school education was however the same.

The effect , for example, was that an applicant with a C and D attainment in the English system would be rejected for entry to an English University but would be accepted by a Scottish one. This helped to fill the vacancies in certain Scottish Universities so these applicants were welcomed. In Engineering this helped sustain several University programmes which might otherwise have had to close.

Engineering was not a popular subject to study among the general UK student applicant body (it was thought to be "rather difficult").

Social studies was becoming more popular and such Departments were mushrooming everywhere especially in the New University sector.

I pressed on somewhat overwhelmed and overawed by this new environment but I knew something about what mattered in the world and was not put off by the difficulties placed in my path.

Students in their Engineering Honours year were required to carry out an individual project chosen from a list based on staff specialism and area of activity. I submitted topics based on my Friction, Lubrication and Wear (aka Tribology) background.

This was the research side of the job. A University lecturer was expected to carry out work in three areas namely teaching, research and administration. I was starting to discover, because no one took me aside and explained it, that the most important of these three was research. Also it was becoming clear that my colleagues were not working as a team on research. One or two were doing some good work but as a "one man band" Typically these individuals got overwhelmed with teaching and administrative load and their research petered out or stagnated..

I had surveyed this area with a view to selecting a topic which would not be over complex in nature nor require expensive experimental equipment. I had seen too much of studies which got bogged down in complex and lengthy experiments.

I chose Wear as an area of study as it was one which I did not know much about and would fill out my Tribology knowledge.

Carbon fibre had recently been developed and was one of the new materials. I started to work with my colleague Ian Fitzpatrick on incorporating carbon into white metal bearing material. Plastics also were of interest represented by such types as Acetal and PTFE.

I designed a wear machine comprising a rotating shaft against which samples of material could be pressed and their loss of mass measured. I had two of these machines manufactured in the Department workshop and carried out preliminary work.

The test sample could be dry or lubricated. Wear was measured by loss of mass after rubbing for typically 1 million revolutions. These machines would serve well as experimental equipment supporting Honours student projects.

I also did research work on lubricants with departmental colleague John Spence. John had been doing work on the rheology of fluids with a former member of staff John Harris.

Harris had left the Department before I got there but his rheology equipment was still in the Department. This comprised a rheogoneometer which was an instrument that measured the rheology of a fluid specimen trapped between a static and revolving circular plate i.e disc. This measured the viscous resisting torque and the force tending to separate the discs the latter being known as "normal force". John's work did not seem to be proceeding in any direction of interest to me and I suggested to him that we could work on the study of lubricants and this led to a project on the performance of the multi-grade motor engine lubricant. Multi-grade oils had first been marketed to address the oil leakage problem on the Austin Mini engines of the late 1950's.

Engine oil gets thinner as its temperature increases and therefore leaks more readily through cracks. Austin's remedy was to design an oil which would retain a higher viscosity when hot. This was achieved by adding e.g. a styrene monomer plastic material to the oil. Thus the viscosity performance at cold and hot would be stated as e.g. SAE 20-50.

This stated that the oil would have the viscosity of a SAE 20 oil at a low temperature and that of a SAE 50 oil at a higher temperature.

It was a successful product which satisfied the users' need but the question was "Does the multigrade effect deteriorate with use?"

We set up a project in co-operation with the Dundee Police, the Post Office and some staff cars. Certain vehicles would have their oil viscosity sampled when newly filled and monitored thereafter till the oil was changed. We got together enough data to publish a paper at a Tribology conference in Nottingham.

Now that was fine but one was not necessarily measured on achievement nor on published achievement but on *funded* published achievement. We did try to get funding council support but were not successful. There were clearly areas of research which would be favourably considered but ours was not one of them at that time.

Success in academic research is best achieved by sensing the popular topic and by having a research record to support an application. "Popular" could be based on current observed needy national solutions or observed as important by the vetting committee. Our Department was not performing adequately in this area and what was worse was that the staff did not seem to be aware of this. Success lay in having a "publications machine" which would produce results leading to papers on funded research on a continuous basis.

This was a Science based concept which was being foisted on the Engineering discipline and had been commonly practiced in the USA. That culture was gradually being adopted in the UK system. An analogy can be seen in the novel "Changing Places" by David Lodge where he observes a similar UK/USA difference but in the Social Sciences. In the USA model research there is an environment in which research is considered to be much more important than teaching. John and I were trying but not achieving enough.

In 1970 professor Dick became unwell and was in hospital. Sadly his health deteriorated and he died. The department was without a leader and an interim head had to be appointed. Principal Drever nominated Dr Hall and he was to be acting head for a couple of years. It was suspected, cynically, that University administrations took their time over filling vacancies as this must have saved money. I was later to learn that a more sinister reason lay behind the delay in the appointment of a successor to professor Dick. This came to light some time later when I was speaking to our then External Examiner who had been on the appointing committee. He informed me that at the time, following Professor Dicks death, the University was seriously considering not filling the post. This would have suggested that the future of the Department was in doubt. At this time the days of generous University government funding were coming to an end and in Academic council meetings the Principal talked of "Deficit financing" as a fact of life that we would all have to live with. For some time we in the Department had to live with an uncertain future.

Our daughter Caroline was born at Dundee Royal Infirmary on 1st October 1971. I collected Florence and Caroline at DRI in our Morris Minor car.

Arch Hall stepped into the post of acting head of department and this was to last for more than two years. One of the important developments during this time was the grant of funds by Government to allow purchase of a numerically controlled machine tool no doubt as a means of impressing new technology on University Departments.

Ben Robb and I looked at specs of several machines and settled on a Cincinnati NC milling machine. This was a step change in

217

technology and was to provide an impetus to the study of computer based engineering.

In 1972 Alan Barr, then a senior lecturer at Edinburgh University, was seen visiting the Department and was subsequently appointed as professor of Mechanical Engineering.

Alan Barr was a pleasant type of person who was idealistic, fair and liberal in his outlook and dealings with his staff but he did see the need for change if the Department was to survive. The weakness in research was one which he set out to address.

Alan was a theoretical engineering academic with a special interest in vibrations of structures. His idea was to build a team of staff who would support this line of research and to this end he was successful in bringing Ian Davidson and David Watt on board to pursue projects in that area. John Spence followed afterwards.

Another co-worker in the field of Tribology at this time was Ian Fitzpatrick. Ian had set up a Materials Science laboratory which had much metallurgical equipment including microscopes, specimen polishing tables and supporting chemicals etc.

I suggested to him that we should look at the then new carbon fibre technology with a view to using it in bearing material applications. This proposal had its source in the knowledge that the large turbo generators then being manufactured were having problems with the bearing material softening and migrating ie being deformed. My idea was to reinforce the metal with the ultra strong carbon fibres.

We did this by incorporating the fibre into metal powder and extruding it under high pressure through a die. We achieved this and the resulting matrix showed an improved wear life. This work should have been pursued and research council funding sought

218

but we did not think that way and this was a major fault that plagued the MechEng Department. Stronger guidance on applications for SRC (Science Research Council) funding the future of the Department may have been more assured.

The academic benefit from these projects was positive however and many Honours students were given projects with a sound applications theme.

A distraction from research work was placed before us in the shape of industrial R&D (research and development). The University set up an industrial liaison office with a manager, John McLaren as ILO (industrial liaison officer), whose job it was to encourage and nurture cooperation between the University and industry. Before long a meeting of the department was called in which the ILO presented a requirement from a local engineering company who wished a machine designed to manufacture a drilled product. This was to be a special purpose drilling machine. The company also wanted to harness any new technology in the proposed machine.

McLaren made a short presentation of the requirement and the response was muted or rather non-existent. I had had some experience in dealing with the company and was wary of this being a non project and simply a way of getting us to come up with ideas which they would accept or reject. I also had experience of jig and tool design and so I gave a guarded answer, essentially asking if the company was prepared to come up with funding for the project. McLaren said that it was indeed willing to fund the project. My weakness was that I could not resist the challenge of a design requirement.

I met McLaren after the meeting and said that there would have to be an Electrical Engineering input as modern technology was

219

moving in a digital control direction with special motors likely to be used. I nominated fellow academic staff member Finlay Philip of Electrical Engineering Dept (EE) as a likely contributor based upon his practical knowledge and his study interests. A meeting was arranged at the firm's works and Finlay and I got down to drawing up a proposal. We decided upon a numerically controlled machine using stepping motors to drive the axes of motion. The project was to drill an array of holes at an angle on a circular segment of wood or aluminium.

I designed the machine structure and moving axes which would largely have to be made in workshops and Finlay designed the electrical drive systems based on the Unimatic company's products.

Eventually after several meetings and months of work the machine was built and various tests carried out in my Tribology laboratory. The systems worked well enough in that the desired motions were achieved and the drilling mechanisms did what they were intended to do. There was a difficulty in the basic cutting requirement which was to drill into a surface at an angle. Despite having drill bushes close the work the drill still tended to wander slightly.

Ideally at this point what was needed was a development technician to tweak the basic parameters of the design to get better work and that was where the project was somewhat unsatisfactory. As Finlay and I saw it we had delivered what we set out to do but McLaren did not foresee the amount of development such a project would require. The machine was delivered to the company premises and they put one of their technicians on it and product was produced. The end result was that the company continued to use their existing machines which gave a higher production rate. But we had introduced digital control into their firm and further developments would take place based on the experience gained albeit not with Finlay and I as the providers.

This project had been challenging, informative, improving and enjoyable but it did require a concentration of mind and effort which eclipsed the lubrication and wear work. This project had also to be done while delivering a teaching load.

In 1974 I applied for funding to allow a visit to Dusseldorf where the IMechE Energy group were holding a conference on Energy use in industry. This proved to be a valuable experience and highlighted some of the great energy waste then going on worldwide. It was also my first experience of Germany which was emerging after a ruinous war which however had allowed many of its industries to start again with updated equipment and outlook.

I had suffered from digestive problems since the early 1960's and had been diagnosed with a stomach ulcer during my year at Strathclyde. Various antacids were prescribed which I chose not to continue using. The symptoms of stomach pain would return from time to time and I suspected they were stress related.

In 1982 or thereby I saw a TV programme in which John Mills the film star spoke of his stomach problem and how it was cured by following the Hay system. This system is based on separating protein and starch in meals. I tried it and it worked for me and I have tried to apply it since. I believe it helped me survive the coming storm of the mid 1980's.

I did try to fit into Professor Alan Barr's team of research staff who were working on various aspects of Vibration. As far as I could see Alan's work was focused on trying to describe how an elemental structural body, e.g. a beam, would behave under vibration. This work included parametric vibration which was associated with the various modes of motion the beam might adopt. However I just could not see my way into this somewhat micro-field of study. I was much more interested in macro engineering behaviour and the real world. This of course made me feel outside the work of the Department but I knew what I wanted to do and it was not mathematical analysis of vibrating elements. I did visit the Royal Naval Construction R&D site at Rosyth with a view to working on a project in their area of interest. I did not find anything on which I could make a contribution and had to report this to Alan who was not amused. I decided to stick to my Design and Tribology interests and make the best of it.

Arch Hall retired in the mid 1970's and this meant that third year Design would have to be taken on by other staff. I was expecting to do this and let another do second year Design which I was by then lecturing. Peter Cave joined the Department about this time and his interests were in electronics applied to engineering systems which was a subject later to become generally known as Mechatronics.

It was agreed that Peter would take third year for two years and we would then swop over duties in that subject. Peter introduced microcomputers to the Department which assisted greatly the task of producing Numerical Control programmes for the Cincinnati NC milling machine. These early microcomputers were programmed in a low level language which was less user friendly than today's methods but was a great advance on the teleprinter machines we were then using to produce punched tape as input to the Cincinnati miller. Imagine writing a programme for the miller, which might run to hundreds of lines of code, in which errors could not be amended. That was the teleprinter method. Microcomputers allowed an editor to be employed to see the code produced "soft" and make corrections. Also there was no graphic check that the geometry being programmed was correct and later developments of the microcomputer and software would allow creation of a graphical representation of the planned geometry.

This was in the mid 1970's before the debut of the Commodore Pet computer in 1977 which was the first of the mass produced public desktop computers. I first saw one at an engineering exhibition in the late 1970's and the Commodore stand was so crowded with interested admirers that I could not get near enough to see the computer.

As I remember the RAM was 8kb. Input tape was like an audio magnetic tape used in portable tape players.

Peter also purchased a PDP8 mini-computer from one of his research projects for more weighty work and this proved a success with undergrads and postgrads. Nine inch floppy disks were the firmware used. This level of computer allowed a graphic representation of the planned cutter path to be seen.

The most powerful calculations were made on the then current University mainframe computer the DEC10 which could have data input using IBM punched cards or the new terminal input option. This computer allowed the use of software to carry out finite element analysis (PAFEC) which allowed stress analysis of complex structures using numerical analysis methodology. Ken Peebles in Civil Engineering (CE) and I were pioneering this work in our respective departments.

This was the introduction to computers applied to Engineering which would lead to the new discipline of Computer Aided Engineering (CAE).

Initially I did not get along with Peter but as time passed our aims converged and things progressed from then. Peter left the Department in 1980 to take up a senior lectureship at the then Plymouth Polytechnic which left a gap which would never really be filled.

In 1980 I was asked by Professor Barr to assist with a project that the Ferranti company was proposing in the field of optical fibre communications. This work would involve investigating the practicability of a design of connector for optical fibre. This was a challenging task which would lead to a visit to Berne Switzerland, with Florence, and a visit to Berlin to a course on Optical Fibre technology. The project had a useful outcome and I had a good experience in a new field of study.

In 1977 Principal Drever had retired and the new Principal was Adam Neville professor of Civil Engineering at University of Leeds. He was born in Poland and in WW2 after invasion by the Russians he escaped a labour camp and made his way to Persia to join the Free Polish Forces under British command where he was much decorated for valour. He had had several academic posts and was a specialist in concrete properties.

Meanwhile the progress of electronic computing was accelerating at an unbelievable pace. Alan Newell was appointed to the new Chair of Microcomputing in the Department of Electrical Engineering.

In 1983 an Electronics colleague Alec Dickie approached me to alert me to the "exploding" microcomputing business with a view to getting a Faculty wide computing network set up. He had

224

learned that there was a Government initiative to support the introduction of computers into University Engineering courses which would mean grant in aid to Universities to buy Departmental computing systems. This was of interest to me since computer aided design (CAD) was emerging as a design draughting tool and it was necessary to be on top of developments including computer aided manufacture. (CAM). Alec saw that the Electrical Engineering Department (EE) also had a CAD/CAM imperative for the design of silicon based microelectronic circuits.

Ken Peebles was informed of our plans and he lent his support to seeking a joint CAD system for the Engineering Departments. Alec and I with interested others formed a CAD/CAM system procurement committee which had the support of the Engineering Professoriate but it was Alec and I who did most of the groundwork. This involved visiting round to see what others were doing and what hardware and software options there were.

In January 1984 Ben Robb Senior Scientific Officer in the UoD Mech Eng Department died after a battle with cancer. This was a great loss to me as Ben was a supportive, able and level headed colleague and a good man.

In June 1984 in the midst of this CAD/CAM business I decided to visit the USA to see for myself what was doing over there. I took Florence and our daughters, Fiona and Caroline, with a view to visiting East Coast campuses. We stayed with my cousin Nancy Langan in Linden NJ from where I visited Stevens University in Hoboken and Rutgers University which is the New Jersey State University. We hired a car and drove to University of Maryland near Washington DC and then on to Virginia Polytechnic Institute at Blacksburg staying with Prof. Dean Mook and family.

This was a great trip for us and I did learn something of developments in CAD/CAM in the USA. As far as I could see the Universities there were well endowed with hardware much of which was given free by the American manufacturers such as Digital Equipment Corp.(DEC) or IBM. Use of that hardware with state of the art software was not evident in undergrad courses however.

Stevens U was tooling up with a batch of new mini computers, Rutgers had some home-grown CAD systems in development, Maryland was not there yet but did have some "Basic" CAD programmes in use and VPI was probably the most advanced in the application of CAD CAM and computer aided engineering (CAE). At VPI I had planned a meeting with Professor Mitchell who was a co-author with Joe Shigley of our selected course text *Mechanical Engineering Design.*

After this meeting over lunch I was making my way back to my car and was sheltering from a sudden downpour when a man sidled up to me and asked if I was a visitor to VPI. I explained my interest and he turned out to be the Head of Department of Mechanical Engineering at VPI and he said that they were currently running a short course on CAD/CAM and asked if I would I like to attend the final session on the Saturday morning. I gladly accepted the invitation and joined a group of attendees which comprised industrial types and a few graduates of VPI. The talks were up to date but it was evident that CAD/CAM was not yet in the undergraduate curriculum but soon would be.

The overall conclusion was that CAD/CAM was just entering the USA University curricula at postgrad level with some basic programming aids at undergraduate level.

The UK situation was not much different but was hardware limited as much as anything. Nottingham University had developed the PAFEC software for stress analysis and had then produced a CAD package called DOGS (Drawing Office Graphics System). This software licence was being offered to Universities at a modest annual fee subsidised by the University Grants Committee. This was a fair result as Nottingham had had Government funding to develop the software.

Then occurred the bombshell of Professor Barr intimating his departure from UoD for Aberdeen. Principal Adam Neville had been creating changes in the University since his appointment in 1977 with restructuring developing over the years and Mechanical Engineering (Mech Eng) was to experience his pruning. Alan Barr had crossed swords with Neville who lost no time in setting about the demise of the Department on receiving Alan Barr's resignation. Departments of Geology, English, and Medical Biophysics had already been closed.

There was a spirited attempt by Mech Eng staff to gather support from other staff to resist motions to close Mech Eng. This was to be seen in debates in the Senate on the motion to close. Faculty Engineering staff held meetings to debate the situation and heartening support was evident. But this was noted and ultimately Neville got his way and instructions were given to stop undergraduate recruitment forthwith. There was definitely a reluctance among many staff to be seen to openly support Mech Eng.

The other Engineering professors and some senior staff grouped together to see what could be done to salvage the situation. Alan Newell then Dean of Engineering and Applied Science and Civil Engineering senior lecturer Malcom Horner stood out as seeking a

227

positive solution; Brian Makin was in a difficult position as he was then a member of University Court and probably constrained to follow the official line.

Meanwhile it was evident that the digital age was advancing on the back of developments in computer technology and performance. Despite the turmoil I was determined to see that computer systems were identified and procured for the Engineering Faculty.

The CAD/CAM committee, which I was chairing by this time, had had a promise of funding to set up a Faculty CAD/CAM system and we set about trying to specify a system and recommend it to the Faculty. To this end in addition to my USA visit I visited Huddersfield Polytechnic and saw what Lee Dove was achieving with the Computervision CAD system. This was a very expensive option but its performance was impressive. I also visited Middlesborough Polytechnic where they were having some success with CAD being used in undergraduate work. Both of these systems would have used DEC, IBM or PDP type computers serving a terminal network.

On Allan Barr's departure Dean Alan Newell was appointed interim Head of the Mech Eng Department and we staff in Mech Eng were each asked to submit details of our professional experience and work and achievements at the University to date and we were also asked to propose a new course structure for Mech Eng should it be possible to continue. There was feverish work on this proposed course syllabus which included discussion with the chairman of the Institution of Mechanical Engineers' Education committee and study of the more advanced courses in the UK. The proposals were examined but found to be "not much different from the status quo" despite a significantly increased Electronics content. Dean Alan Newell tried to make a last stand case for certain members of the Mech Eng staff but this was thrown out by the Principal and Dean Newell was divested of his headship of Mech Eng and Professor Brian Makin appointed interim Head of Department. Brain Makin made some suggestion about the future of Mech Eng to the principal but was peremptorily told "I do not wish to hear about Mechanical Engineering".

In the midst of this maelstrom I was contacted by the Professor of Mechanical Engineering at Edinburgh University Joe McGeough who asked if I could meet him on neutral territory to discuss the situation. We met over afternoon tea in the St James hotel in Edinburgh where I brought him up to date with the situation as far as I could without breach of confidence. He proposed the case for an East of Scotland Mechanical Engineering Department based on Edinburgh, Dundee and Aberdeen Universities. This was radical thinking but may have had mileage so after some further discussion I agreed to take the idea back to Dundee. I put the idea to Alan Newell but he was quick to say that it would not be acceptable in the current circumstances. He implied that Principal Neville was determined to close Mechanical Engineering down and no such scheme would have a chance of success.

Things were looking bad and soon we Mech Eng staff were called to a meeting with Principal Neville where he told us that Mechanical Engineering would close.

Shortly thereafter we were individually contacted with an appointment with Vice Principle William Stewart to give us details of our severance from the University. We were fortunate that it was Professor Stewart who had this task which he carried out with consideration and humanity.

The apparent course "image" the Principal and Engineering professors were looking for was a course based on Electronics applied to Mechanical Engineering and allegedly the new course proposals did not match up to this concept.

Simultaneously with all of this intrigue an ambitious scheme by the engineering professors was being cooked up to get money to establish an Institute of Computer Aided Engineering and Manufacture (ICAEM). This Institute would cooperate with industry and bring funded research projects to the University.

It so happened that the CAD/CAM work Alec Dickie and I were working on fell nicely into this description. My hand was therefore strengthened by this ICAEM development.

When it came my turn to see Professor Stewart there was no mention of my appointment being terminated. The CAD/CAM committee was to continue with the procurement of a CAD system which would be used by the Departments of Engineering for academic, research and industrial funded project work.

Sadly Alec Dickie took seriously ill with a brain tumour about this time and had to take medical retirement. He and I had been on a fact finding visit to IBM Greenock when he complained of feeling strange. Some days later he was admitted to hospital.

Professor Brian Makin stepped in and with my help was brought up to speed on our plan.

Electrical Engineering particularly wanted to have a good Microelectronic circuit design and manufacture facility e.g. "Mentor", Mechanical/Manufacturing Engineering would want CAD/CAM/CAE capability and Civil Engineering would want CAD/CAE capability. [CAD is Computer-aided-design, CAM is

Computer-aided-manufacture and CAE is Computer-aided-engineering.]

Before Alec Dickie's illness he had highlighted the Apollo computer products. These were different from mainframe or mini mainframe computers in that they had computing power built in to each "terminal" but were connected in a local area network to capacious storage or what seemed capacious at the time. The CAD/CAM committee noted this option and Professor Brian Makin and I visited Apollo's premises in Livingstone to see demonstrations of the kit and speak to Alan Opgard the sales person for Apollo.

I had knowledge of the failings of using a mainframe and dumb terminal to carry out finite element calculations the major one being contention for central processor access i.e. "on line" operation was slow if at all available and programmes had to be put through a queuing process i.e. submit your programme and come back some hours later, or tomorrow, for the output. This would not do for CAD which was a hands on interactive process with the need for instant results.

With the Apollo approach "intelligent" terminals were actually mini computers with all of 1Mb RAM (Random access memory) and were ideal for CAD and later CAM and CAE. While there was some support for desktop microcomputers to be used they were *at the time* nowhere near powerful enough to carry the emerging proprietary CAD systems. It was agreed to settle for the Apollo approach and Brian Makin set about getting the best deal for the University. There was not much room for negotiation as there were no real competitors in the field.

The order was for ten Apollo computers with 12 inch screens (black and white) and two with 16 inch screens (colour). These

231

would be set up as a local area network with proper computer desks and a central storage device. This hardware would open the door to undergraduate class use of CAD systems and more.

A computer system manager (Tony Gowland ex NCR) was appointed to run the system and co-ordinate its use in the Faculty of Engineering and Applied Science.

With the system installed I was able to get the Pafec suite of programmes installed. Pafec had been chosen by the University Grants committee for an all-Universities deal which made the software affordable to all.

My plan was that Honours students would do the pioneer work and second and third year students would follow.

The Mechanical Engineering course was now on its way out as students worked through the years the last graduating in 1989. It should be noted that there were a good number, 70 to 80,of funded places that were not filled due to axing of Mech Eng intakes. If these are valued at £8000 each there was an annual loss of income to the University of approximately £640,000.

The "management" whoever they were, but definitely led by Principal Neville, then decided that the way forward was with Manufacturing Engineering. This was based on an article in the technical press to the effect that what the UK really needed was Manufacturing Engineers. To this end the post of Professor of Manufacturing Engineering was advertised after the setting up of a new Department..

The Principal or his advisers then came up with the idea to abolish the Faculty of Engineering and Applied Science and incorporate the Engineers into a new Faculty of Science and Engineering. With the expansion of Life Sciences as a policy decision it was clear that the Engineers would be the poor relations in the new Faculty. Electrical Engineering and Electronics would however be protected. The new entity of Manufacturing Engineering would be subsumed in a new Department viz Applied Physics and Electronics and Manufacturing Engineering (APEME).

This new Department was to be headed by the very able Physicist Peter LeComber who along with Professor Speir had established a strong research group working on amorphous silicon.

In June 1987 Bernard Hon was appointed to the chair of Manufacturing Engineering. He was then at Birmingham University and had a research background in spark erosion machining. He would join Dundee University and bring with him his research team. His able lieutenant was Hossam Ismail who would get a lecturer post. There were other research associates and assistants also joining on a contract basis. Hossam was keen on microcomputers and showed interest in my then desktop machine which was an NCR product.

The Mechanical degree course was working its way out by then with most staff relocated or early retired with part time posts. I was then the only full time member of the Academic staff of the Mechanical Engineering Department. One of my jobs was to seek part time staff to fill the holes in provision.

One of Bernard Hon's first jobs during the coming 1977-8 session was to design the new course in Manufacturing Engineering. There were only a few Manufacturing Engineering Departments in the UK. Management principles and manufacturing techniques would form a major part of the degree structure. There was to be a, nearly, common first year for Manufacturing, Electrical and Electronics and Physics students.

As time went by it became clear that there was not a large undergraduate demand for Manufacturing Engineering.

In 1978 Principal Neville completed a second 5 year term and decided to retire from the academic administrative business. He had presided during exciting times.

The new Principal was Michael Hamlin from Birmingham University where he was a professor in Civil Engineering specializing in water resource engineering.

It takes a year or so before a new principal starts to make changes.

The Manufacturing Engineering degree got going and we had our first intake in 1989 as the last Mechanical Engineering students finished their Honours year.

After a couple of years of this new set-up I had a meeting scheduled with Bernard Hon about some course matter and when he arrived in his room he said "That's it, he can get another boy" I sat there wondering what this was about and it seemed he had just been to see the principal so I guess that his dissatisfaction arose from that meeting. I never really discovered what had happened but I suspect that it had something to do with resurrecting Mechanical Engineering.

The fact was that Mechanical Engineering had had a useful intake of 15 – 25 students per year with most surviving to honours year so approximately 80 FTEs (fulltime equivalent credits) and this revenue had gone. Manufacturing engineering student uptake had not been good and I presume that Principal Hamlin asked Bernard to bring back Mechanical Engineering. Bernard had also been having difficulty with getting, as he saw it, a fair share of the (APEME) Departmental resources for his degree course and was already dissatisfied.

234

Amidst all this I decided to attend one of Bernard's weekly research group meetings. I felt that I should get more involved in the Manufacturing Engineering research activities so I wanted to hear his various research workers reports. Bernard opened the meeting by stating that he had given notice that he would be leaving the University.

It would be an understatement to say that a stunned silence followed.

He never said what caused him to resign. He was the typical Chinese in that respect i.e. inscrutable. Neither Bernard or Hossam had shown much interest in the Apollo mini computer network. Not his idea perhaps - so ignored it.

In fact the system had been a success and I had undergraduates doing CAD/CAM/CAE in their project work probably ahead of any institution in the UK.

I was able to gauge this at a CAE conference in Glasgow and at another in Nottingham where Perkins Engines were at the time ie late 1980's leading the field in applying CAD/CAE in industry.

Bernard Hon left to take up a chair of Manufacturing at Liverpool University ca 1990 and we never heard from him again. It was a pity Bernard chose to leave as he was a dynamic personality who was aware of the state of the art in Manufacturing Engineering.

It was clear to me that survival in the University system was dependent on the funded research activity of a department and of the individual staff member.

So what was going on with regard to research work during this time?.

Brian Makin as the acting Head of the Mechanical Engineering Department asked staff to propose research projects which might receive funding from NCR. I suspect that NCR heard that the Department was under threat and made such funds available.

I had been looking at Expert Systems and thought that this would have applications in the Design field. Much was being said about the topic but little was being achieved. My proposal was accepted among others from Electrical Engineering then I had to find a researcher to help carry out the work.

The post was advertised and people were interviewed. The person recruited for my project was, let's say, Rachel, a computing science graduate. She was a disappointment as a research assistant and seemed determined not to fit into a teamwork regime or any kind of disciplined approach to the project. Any way I soldiered on in an environment of chaotic dismemberment of the Mechanical Engineering Department. At the end of the one year project she had produced little but we were able to put on a demo of sorts for the NCR engineer involved namely Ian Campbell then head of document handling engineering. One learns from one's mistakes and this had been a classic case. Expert Systems were, at the time, too immature a subject to have gone into but one conclusion which resulted was that computer system power of the time was woefully inadequate to make applications of any worth in practice. By 2017 workstation computers were much more powerful and no doubt we shall see more of Expert Systems in the future.

Another lesson learned was not to hire an assistant to do something that one was not proficient to do oneself.

However other irons were in the fire. Sheikh Guendouse a graduate from Algeria applied to study Computer Aided Design and Manufacture and I offered to supervise his work in that area.

236

We were able to produce a working system which converted engineering drawing information into a manufacturing programme for manufacture directly from the CAD drawing. This was encouraging.

Ian Campbell had also put to me several possible project ideas for solution and I put these up for Honours project topics. Julia Clayton chose the topic of Document Handling for her Honours project. There were several challenges to work on including cold temperature operation, document properties and alternative document handling methods. This was a successful project in many ways and produced useful outcomes.

It was so much more productive to have an assistant who had studied engineering and had the correct attitude to work and reporting. I had three other Honours students working on projects also so the lab was humming with activity. I won funding from NCR to support a research assistant for one year and Julia Clayton accepted the challenge. Apart from a reasonable salary she could enrol as an Master of Science postgraduate student. This project developed some of the ideas from her Honours project and was an all-round success including for her an MSc degree.

This was a model for further successful research projects and a similar path was trodden by Wayne Cowpland and Ian McLenaghan.

Mechanical Engineering would seemingly be on its way back though progress on this would be slow. Peter LeComber was still APEME head of Department and would soon pass the headship to Arthur Cracknell also a Physicist.

When Arthur took over the job he spoke to me about the Mfg/MechEng course. Arthur was having to handle the departure of Bernard Hon and would be depending on my help to keep things going until the replacement professor took over.

In the meantime academic staff had been appointed for the Manufacturing Engineering degree course. Mark Pridham joined us from Nottingham University, Gareth Thomson from CAV Ltd, and Paul Lewis from Newcastle. Sheikh Meeran had been working in aircraft engineering in India and France.

I also recruited part time staff including Dr Lord Robert Mercer Nairne, with experience of industrial management, and Joe Lowrie the latter a former Chief Designer with Timex Ltd and also formerly of British Leyland Bathgate.

Simultaneously with the planned demise of Mechanical Engineering I had been carrying out work for the NCR company in Dundee which is a precision engineering manufacturer notably of the Auto Teller machine. This work had gone well and the cooperative venture was assisted greatly by the good offices of Ian Campbell who had been one of our students on course when I joined Dundee University in 1968 and incidentally the only student to have scored 100% in one of my examinations..

This project work put me in a position to introduce two of the Engineering Professors to NCR viz Brian Makin and Alan Newell then Dean of the Faculty of Engineering and Applied Science. These two famously did not get on with each other, (Tweedledee Alan and Tweedledum Brian?) and I was somewhat surprised to find that I had better connections with local industry than they did -but it was so. I was happy to be a neutral go between and just got on with it.

It was important to the University to be seen to be actively cooperating with a firm which was in the computerized machine industry.

I proposed a piece of work to NCR on document handling engineering which was one of their core competencies. I had had one of the last honours students working in this area (Julia Clayton) when I won £30,000 project funding. This upset the ICAEM (Institute of Computer aided Engineering and Manufacture) manager as they were supposed to be bringing in the projects. However I had simply applied enterprise and salesmanship had the necessary contacts and experience to go it alone, but for the good of the APEME Department of course.

NCR set up an offsite research lab in the Fulton building under the management of the able NCR engineer Norrie Taylor. This was a properly run and funded lab which did work on the various aspects of ATM technology. I was awarded several contracts to pursue during its tenure. It lasted from 1988 to 1998 when NCR opened their new Technology centre on Kingsway West near their factory. By the time the University lab closed in 1998 I had attracted approximately £250,000 of funding for my own projects for NCR.

In the midst of these developments tragedy occurred when Peter Lecomber died while on holiday in Switzerland. This was a disastrous loss for the Department of APEME as Peter was a pillar of research strength in the area of amorphous silicon properties and applications.

The Department of APEME decided that it would be a good idea to appoint a senior lecturer in Mechanical and Manufacturing engineering and this was advertised.

Arthur Cracknell (head of department) drew me aside after a meeting and indicated that he would like me to apply. He wanted to see my application before submitting it.

Arthur was very good at gauging what University Appointment boards looked for and he was able to make helpful suggestions which I very much appreciated.

I had a few published papers but not a great deal since most of my work had been in association with industry. I included a list of some 43 consultancies which I had performed since joining the University.

It has to be understood here that my view of useful research and development was that which was done to improve a real product, process or our understanding of it. It was this I had pursued since graduating and I was comfortable with that. This was not ideal behaviour in the eyes of the University. What mattered to University types was research funding from the appropriate grants body such as the Science Research Council. While my application was supported by industrial and academic referees I did not impress them enough to warrant appointment. However their favoured applicant withdrew and I was appointed after all.

The plan now was to re-introduce Mechanical Engineering to run alongside manufacturing Engineering and Management.

Michael Hamlin was still the Principal and I credit him with the proposal to re-introduce Mechanical Engineering at Dundee.

Bernard Hon had left with his retinue of research staff and clearly we would have to find staffing for the Manufacturing Engineering and Management (MEM) degree and the new Mechanical Engineering degree. In addition student numbers were not good for the MEM degree and it was likely to be phased out.

The fact was that students were more attracted to a Mechanical Engineering degree which opened more doors of opportunity than did MEM. It was important that our degree courses be accredited by the appropriate Professional Institution and the Institution of Mechanical Engineers was sounded out for advice. Dundee had had this accreditation till 1990 when the previous MechEng degree closed. It was made clear that accreditation would depend on IMechE being convinced of the University's commitment to the degree e.g. appointing a professor of Mechanical Engineering.

Several applications for the post were received but one stood out as being most suitable. This was Jim Hewit of Loughborough University. Jim would be in his early 50's and was looking for a chair in native Scotland. After visiting and interview Jim was appointed.

Jim moved in and brought some research students and his favourite technician Alan Slade. Jim's area of research was in automation and in particular computers applied to machine control.

So things were starting to look better and we were successful in getting the MechEng degree accredited by IMechE. My research work with NCR continued to be robust but would tail off at the end of the 1990's as NCR moved to a more in-house laboratory at their new Technology centre.

Student numbers were growing with the re-establishment of the MechEng degree and the MEM degree was allowed to work out and then withdrawn. It was decided that Mechanical Engineering was gaining in strength and could stand alone again. I was coordinating the Mechanical Degree programme while Jim Hewit built up a sound research base. Eric Abel who had been running the postgraduate Bio-Engineering course joined Mechanical Engineering.

For my part new opportunities for research funding were not good and would have meant pursuing new avenues.

I had by this time (1999) been in engineering for 44 years and was considering that if the opportunity arose I would leave the University service. This indeed arose with early retirement schemes being offered to release staff if they wished. I negotiated a deal to retire at 2000 and work part time for a further three years to 2003. In fact it became 2004 after I was asked to do a further year.

There comes a point when one has been in a job for a long time that a change would be a relief. Professor Jim Hewit said something of the sort when he told me he would not mind being a bus driver for while. I knew what he meant. The terms of my retirement were attractive and would allow Florence and I to have more holidays and cruises. The time was right and I chose the retirement deal and left the University in August 2004.

Thus far 16 years of retirement has been mostly enjoyable. I have volunteered in the Dundee City Archives where I assist in cataloguing and interpreting engineering aspects of the collections which induced me to write the book "Caledon Ships" based on the Caledon photographic collection. Regular golf has been played but is now on the wane as my fellow playing group gave up the game.

Florence and I are regular dancers, in the old fashioned way. We have completed 25 cruises to date and look forward to many more.

Gardening and regular walks help to keep up ones fitness and it is our intention to "Keep on dancing".

Grangemouth Petrochemical Plant

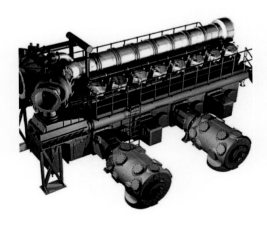

Gas Engine Compressor

Variable rotational speed rig

Engine rig for telemetry

See image credits p267

Connecting Rod & Telemetry

National Engineering Laboratory- East Kilbride

In the Dundee Law Tunnel 1968

Fulton Building University of Dundee

See image credits p267

University of Dundee Tower 1970's

See image credits p267

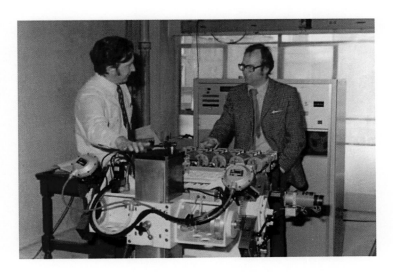

DM and Finlay Philip with NC Drilling machine

247

Florence at Engineers Ball Pitlochry-Atholl Palace Hotel

At the board - a CIRC project – DM, another and Ben Robb

Mechanical Engineering Staff University of Dundee 1968-9

Student cube-collection of students NC work

University of Dundee Mechanical Engineering Dept.
Staff and Students ca 1984

Front Row l to r: Bob Main Chief Technician, Joe Lowrie visiting lecturer, David Middleton lecturer, David Watt lecturer, Hector Hetherington lecturer, Alan Barr Professor, Ross Williamson Senior lecturer, Jim McD Brown lecturer, Bill Borthwick lecturer,

Richard Neilson research student is behind Alan Barr.

3rd row lh side Alec Barnes technician is in front of Lewis Murray technician. At rh end is Angus Howard technician and behind him is Dave Nicol technician.

Mech Eng Grads 1995. Iain McLenaghan mid back row

Colin Jones right end of back row.

DM, Donnie (lh) Robbie (rh), Nancy, Edie Ella Rena
The Middleton siblings 1988

Cruising and still dancing!

Caroline Edward and Fiona

Appendix 1

The Cars

In 1963 as my Honours project work was less demanding than the preceding lecture terms I decided to train for my driving licence. I visited the British School of Motoring in the Queens Park area of Glasgow and booked for a course. The deal was that a course of lessons had to be taken ie not one lesson paid for at a time. I duly turned up at the shop and proceeded with the course. I had a different instructor each time which did not help with identifying weak areas in my driving. The cars used were Ford Anglias.

After about eight lessons I was entered for the test and I was taken in the car to the Driving Examiners office. The examiner was a rather sour faced man and gave me directions to drive. A thunderstorm thereupon began which did not help. The result was that I failed the test. I put this down to not getting practice in driving between lessons.

After finishing at Glasgow I had further lessons in Dundee from an ex policeman who ran a one man driving school again using a Ford Anglia. This was a much better arrangement as he could identify individual weaknesses requiring practice.

I sat the second driving test in August 1963 in Broughty Ferry which was a much more congenial area to be examined in. This time I passed.

Florence and I planned to have a holiday driving around Scotland in August 1963.

Should I hire a car or buy an old car? As I remember I had a rather "student" cavalier attitude at the time and decided on buying an old car. My brother in law Jack Cumming assisted me in looking at a few which were on offer in the Dundee Courier. I settled on a grey Standard Flying 9 of 1937 vintage which cost £15. It needed some tidying up of the front offside wing which I carried out in my other brother in law's (Gerd Bueckardt) workshop in St Salvador Street. Florence and I set off for a short tour taking in Aberdeen returning via Royal Deeside and Braemar. This car was comprehensively worn out and needed constant attention to keep it going. As my course in Birmingham was imminent I stored the car in Gerd's workshop till the Christmas vacation.

On returning from Birmingham I re-taxed and insured the car for the Christmas vacation and set out on the Roads again. Then I discovered that this car did not like the cold weather. It would start and run for a short while then die. It would refuse to start until an hour or so had passed. After that it would run ok for the rest of the day but next day it went through the same process. I sought help from several people but there was no solution found before the time came to return to Birmingham.

When I returned for the Easter vacation and again got the car on the Road the same problem of poor running was found. An MOT test was also due and the car failed with excessive wear on a track rod end. I decided to sell or scrap the car and was offered £5 from Arnotts Auto spares in Guthrie St. Dundee. I advertised the car in the Courier for £10 and eventually sold it for £8 and good riddance. Florence and I went off to the Odeon Cinema and I felt a good sense of freedom from a troublesome problem.

I suspect that the basic problem was a worn out engine with insufficient compression to sustain reliable running. The only further knowledge of this car was in an advertisement in the Courier for a grey Standard Flying 9 in "showroom condition" for £35. Was this my problem car?

The next time a car became desirable was when I was working in Grangemouth at BHC. They advertised the sale of their company car, a Riley Pathfinder. For "offers". I would have gone after this car but the National Commercial Bank would not let me have an overdraft to buy it. As Edward's birth drew near in February 1965 I could see that a car would be desirable for getting around. At the local filling station on the Bo'ness Road there was a 2.2 litre maroon 1958 Humber Hawk for sale "to clear" at £25. I knew this type of car as my sister's husband Jack Cumming had one for years and it was a comfortable and reliable car, mostly. While this car was only seven years old it was clearly suffering from corrosion at the sill level. This was common at the time and I am sure that it was an example of built in obsolescence. I recruited the help of friend and BHC colleague Bob Craig and we took the car for a short test drive. It ran quite well and I liked the roomy luxury of the well worn interior. Bench front seat and column change. I bought the car and undertook the task of refurbishing it. The paint finish was dull and faded which was a feature of the deep maroon colour at that time. However I used a paint cleaner on it and Simoniz polish brightened it up. I got a plate made at BHC to cover a corroded part of the driver's door and without delay ordered a new battery and changed the engine oil

We enjoyed that car for almost 3 years with little trouble. It started and ran in the coldest weather and we had many runs to Dundee from Grangemouth and East Kilbride. This car enabled me to travel to East Kilbride from Grangemouth after I changed jobs allowing me to catch an early train at Falkirk High to Glasgow daily.

On a trip to Dundee Early in 1968 the car failed to start on cold frosty morning.

With the help of Benny Murray, an old friend and my parents' next door neighbour, and a tow from his car, we got the Humber running. It would not however go above thirty five miles per hour but Florence, baby Ed and I set out for East Kilbride and managed to make it without a problem, I decided that was the end of the Humber as serious engine trouble was probably the cause. I sold it for £1 to a Glasgow scrap dealer who came and towed it away and I felt a sense of relief. It had been a good car for us but at 9 years old it was worn out.

We were living in Dundee at Claypotts Castle Gardens when the need for a car raised its head again. I had been fancying a Morris Minor and had bid for a colleague's car when it came up for sale. Having failed at that attempt I saw an ad in the Courier newspaper for a minor at £65 so I went to see it. As it happened it was just round the corner from our home. I had a look at the car which was a 1954 split windscreen model but had had the 1000cc engine and gearbox fitted. I offered £40 for it which was not accepted but later that day the seller contacted me to say I could have it for £40.

This car was older than the Humber but was actually in better condition. The Minor was a well designed car with everything easy to get at and straightforward to repair. I also had expert help when required from my colleague technician Ian Urquhart..

This car served us well even taking us (4 at that time) on holiday to Benderloch near Oban. It was economical, well 30mpg at that time seemed economical. I had to change a clutch and also a pilot bearing but beyond that it was mainly consumables.

The body was slowly breaking up due to rust and there was always something needing welded to pass the MoT test. I bought my elder brother Robert's car, a 1.5 litre Morris Oxford, and sold the Minor for what I paid for it three years earlier.

The Morris Oxford (5533 SP) I bought in 1971 was the Farina type of 1962 manufacture and was a two tone light green / dark green colour. It had a bench front seat with a column change. This was a well made car which gave little trouble other than slowly rusting away underneath and some breakout on the body. At £75 it was a good buy and we needed the bigger car as there were now 5 of us. This car had been the exhibited car at the 1962 Scottish Motor Show in the Kelvin hall Glasgow where the original owner had bought it off the stand. My brother had been the second owner.

We had several holidays in the Oxford travelling to Bournemouth all the way by Road and also by the Motorail from Perth. That model suffered from front shock absorbers of limited life which manifested itself in a rocking pitching motion at speed. New shockers were fitted with little difficulty. Economy was similar to the Minor and the engine was quite silent on tickover and gave little other trouble other than the replacement of the Bendix starter pinion which was readily changed. This would be the last car we owned which had a starting handle. Rust was invading in several places and it was time to get another car. I chose a Ford Cortina which was a popular car at the time and there would be help and knowledge available for repairs etc.

I sold the Morris for £100 i.e. more than I paid for it but it was a time of high inflation after all.

The Ford Cortina on sale at Whitton motors cost £1300, was a golden brown colour with matching interior trim. This was serious money. It was in apparently good condition but later examination showed signs of body repairs at the front end.

However it ran well enough and it was nice to have individual seats and a slick floor change gearbox. Seatbelts were fitted as standard. Independent suspension all round with McPherson struts on the front. We had several holidays in this car but it was prone to side wind effect on steering especially on the motorway. A clutch, a broken rear coil spring, a strut lower ball joint, an ignition lock core, an overhead camshaft and a rusty headlamp reflector had to be replaced during the car's time with me. This was it seemed a "consumable" car and gave me a poor impression of Ford engineering. A friend, Beryl Fitzpatrick, was selling her company car, a blue Vauxhall Cavalier Mk2 of 1981 vintage, and I jumped at the chance to purchase it for £2000. The Ford was kept for a while for family use but the time came when it had to go for £400.

The 1982 model Cavalier was a base model but Streets ahead of the Ford Cortina in all respects. Everything seemed better engineered and substantial. This was our first transverse engine front wheel drive car. It drove well in slippy wintry conditions due to the extra weight of transmission on the front axle. It was more economical than the Cortina and everything worked and continued to do so, mostly.

As in many cars of the period it had manual choke which required some coaxing especially in cold weather. This would be our last carburettor type fuel system as petrol injection types were beginning to be fitted to family cars. The only major repair was a replacement overhead camshaft.

Care was required when cornering on wet roads as the rear end was liable to slip sideways due to the lighter load at the rear. It is wise to put the best treaded tyres on the rear. In time body corrosion started to show and I was no longer prepared to fight the losing battle of repairing rust damage. Body shop advice was to run the car into the ground. I got the opportunity to buy my nephew's company car which was another, later year, blue Vauxhall Cavalier ca 1985 but a with petrol injection system and higher trim level. The old Cavalier was sold to my daughter and her fiance'.

The second Cavalier was a nice car indeed. It had a more luxurious feel to it and there was no problem in manipulating the choke; there wasn't one. It was a good all-rounder with improved fuel consumption due to its multi-point fuel injection system but there was snag with this model in that the pressurized fuel line from the pump at the rear of the car was liable to fail. This happened when Florence was driving it resulting in a dead engine. The RAC man was called and fixed it promptly by simply cutting the worn part off and re-clipping the flex pipe. After a few years use corrosion was detected on a rear wheel arch and it was time to look for a newer car. A sale was being held of cars at the Citroen dealership in Dundee. There was a maroon Cavalier which had a "Q" car preparation, it was claimed. This was the Vauxhall dealership preparation level and was supposed to be a reliable quality standard. The old Vauxhall was sold to a taxi driver and it was seen for some time after to be giving service around the town.

The third Cavalier was more basic than its predecessor and was found to be less efficient. I found that it had a petrol injection system but only single point rather than an injector to each cylinder. Apart from that it was a good workhorse of a car and it had power steering. In 2001 I fancied having a Rover 75 because of its luxury interior and general looks. It got a good write up in the motoring press and was praised for its sturdy build. I saw one advertised in Alyth at the heritage car company there. We arranged to have a test drive and found it a comfortable car and it looked in good condition. A price just over £10k was agreed and We picked the car up a few days later. The Rover was a lovely car to drive if you liked that limo feel which I did.

It had 10k miles on the clock was silver coloured and had a W plate. We had that car till late 2008 and covered many miles across the UK. It was a 1.8 petrol and the engine did rev a bit at 70mph presumably to get the torque required from an underpowered engine for this car size. Otherwise it was very good until, after a coolant change, I noticed that the coolant level was dropping very slowly. I kept an eye on this for a long time and raised the matter with Arnold Clark in Dundee the main dealer who had supplied the car which was still under warranty. Their view was that it was probably the coolant cap leaking and they said they would order a new one.

That cap never arrived in their store and I suspect that it was a delaying tactic. About this time the Rover company had problems and there was news that the directors had added to their pension funds. Not long after that the company went into administration.

I kept using the Rover 75 usefully and tried the leaky radiator preparations which were for sale. This reduced the loss but did not cure it. Then one day while we were driving to East Lothian the temperature gauge showed overheat and I pulled in to the side of the Road and put in some coolant. This had little effect and I drove the car till it came to a halt. This was the classic blown gasket symptom and the RAC was called and towed the car to our destination where we left it for the garage to look at. The report was seized engine which was going to be a costly job and in excess of the value of the car. I made a deal to sell the car to the garage at a scrap price and that was the end of the Rover for us. I heard later that the car was seen driving around so the engine must have been reconditioned. The interior of that car was superb with a real polished walnut dash and plush interior upholstery. Now carless I researched the car reviews in order to get a more reliable model and settled upon the Toyota Avensis. We travelled to Aberdeen to see an advertised pre -registered 2008 Avensis hatchback and had a trial run. It was agreed that this car would do and we purchased it and called for it a few days later.

This Avensis was a black 2 litre diesel with the 6 speed manual box plus reverse and TR trim. It was a superb car for comfort, low stress driving and lots of extras. In addition it had an overall mpg of 55 and the tyres lasted 35000 miles. I sold the Avensis in September 2019 for £1400. The phone did not stop ringing after advertising the car on Gumtree.

Car reliability was high on the list of properties required of the replacement for the Toyota. Downsizing was also on the list and after trying a few cars the petrol fuelled Honda Jazz SE came top of the list.

This was our first brand new car and the choice of colour was "bright sporty blue". West End Garage of Broughty Ferry was able to give a close match price to that offered on line and so far trading with them has been agreeable. The Jazz is generous in interior space and feels a solid car to drive giving 51mpg to date. It fits into our garage well and leaves more working space at my bench. The deal included 5 years free servicing.

That is the car story so far.

Standard Flying 9 1937

Humber Hawk Mk2 1958

Morris minor (1954) and Morris Oxford (ca 1964)

Ford Cortina Mk 3 (ca 1976) and Morris Oxford

Vauxhall Cavalier Mk 2   1985

Vauxhall Cavalier Mk 3 1996

Rover 75 1.8 2001

Toyota Avensis 2 litre Diesel   2008

Honda Jazz 1.3 SE   2019

Image Credits

The University crests on the back outer cover do not indicate that the respective University sponsors accredits or certifies this publication.

Back cover crests are shown with thanks to and by permission of Universities of Abertay, Birmingham, Strathclyde and the Institution of Mechanical Engineers .

Scotch boiler image credit in Part 2 by kind permission of the International Brotherhood of Boilermakers Kansas City USA.

Images credited to J D Forbes are included courtesy of the late Winnie Cochrane and by permission of Brian McArtney.

The copyright owner of images marked Bedford LeMere, Temple Press and Scottish Aviation have not been found after reasonable and diligent efforts. Credit is hereby given with thanks. This also applies to the compressor, variator and counter images.

Images of telemetry connecting rod, variable speed transmission and engine laboratory cell were published in 1967 and are by courtesy of National Engineering Laboratory.

Image of RCST Glasgow (University of Strathclyde) credit T. Higgins Pinterest with thanks.

Image of Birmingham University Engineering building credit Nigel Makura with thanks.

University of Dundee images of Fulton and Tower buildings reproduced with kind permission of University of Dundee Archive Services.

Grangemouth Petrochemical plant image credit: By User:John, CC BY-SA 3.0, By permission with thanks. https://commons.wikimedia.org/w/index.php?curid=2459867

St Michaels School building image used by kind permission of D.C. Thomson &Co Ltd

INDEX

Engineering my future